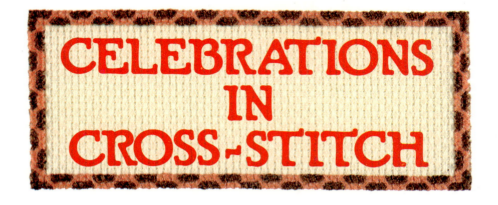

CELEBRATIONS IN CROSS-STITCH

LISBETH PERRONE

SEDGEWOOD PRESS®
New York, N.Y.

To everyone who loves celebrations . . .

ACKNOWLEDGEMENTS

I would like to extend my thanks and deep appreciation to those who made this "Celebration book" possible: to Justine Chicks, Sara Huntington Brown, and Sonja Martensson, who skillfully helped in working the embroideries; to Nilams Glass Service for framing many of the pieces in the book; and to Jackson E. Shirley, Jr. for an outstanding effort in translating my designs into beautiful and clear charts. Finally I would like to thank all of you embroiderers, who are the main source of inspiration and encouragement to me in the creation of these needlework books.

Special thanks to the Swedish Cottage, Liza Siegler, Bob and Ava Siegler, Nancy Sang, and Barbara Melcher for providing some of the charming accessories used in the photographs throughout the book. And special thanks to Dina van Zweck.

Special thanks to Hallmark—Party Accessories. Also to Laura Ashley fabrics, which were used as background in photographs on pages: 25, 35, 43, 47, 81, 89, 112, 115, 130, and 149.

Editorial Director: Dina von Zweck

For Sedgewood Press
Director: Elizabeth P. Rice
Project Manager: Connie Schrader
Project Editor: Sandy Towers
Production Manager: Bill Rose
Photography: Schecter Lee
Design: Remo Cosentino/Bookgraphics

Distributed by Meredith Corporation, Des Moines, Iowa.

ISBN: 0-696-02318-0

Library of Congress Catalog Card Number: 88-061381

Printed in the United States of America
10 9 8 7 6 5 4 3 2 1

CONTENTS

INTRODUCTION

A celebration is a time for rejoicing. Whether it's an established holiday or a birthday, graduation, or housewarming, it's a time for family and friends to gather and enjoy everything that is special about the event. It is a time to set aside whatever is routine and humdrum and create a festive atmosphere.

We have a heritage of wonderful special occasions—and we make them our own by continuing traditional customs as well as giving these customs new, personal interpretations. A celebration calls for splendid food—honeycake and sweet wine . . . barbecue and lemonade . . . or roast turkey with all the trimmings. All are part of our heritage.

Decorations and gift-giving are a mainstay of most holidays. Many holidays have their own distinctive colors and motifs. The soft pastels of Easter are so very different from the striking orange and black of Halloween. And we all, children and grown-ups alike, look forward expectantly to the vibrant red and green of Christmas.

This book is a celebration of celebrations. With over forty cross-stitch projects to choose from, you can create beautifully decorative designs to commemorate your favorite holidays . . . and the very special occasions on which family and friendship are celebrated.

I know you will enjoy this book. It is a treasure trove of needlework possibilities. You can use the designs as you see them here, or you can use your creativity to change them around, bring in your own color combinations, or use your own favorite mottoes and sayings.

Celebrate in cross-stitch—and bring a sense of beauty into every celebration of the year.

Lisbeth

HOW TO USE THIS BOOK

Celebrations in Cross-Stitch is a workbook with over 40 designs for pillows, pictures, hangings, table coverings, place mats, napkins, runners, cards, and accessories. Each design is shown in color and is given its own chart, done in symbols. Each symbol represents one stitch in a certain color. A change of symbol on the chart means a change of color in the design. Blank squares in the charts should be left unstitched unless other instructions are given. Where a chart extends for more than a page, it is indicated how and where to continue on the following page. If only half of a full motif appears on the chart, the chart should be "mirror-imaged." Simply reverse the chart from the center (either from left to right, or top to bottom, or both). To make any of the projects in the book, you need to be familiar with only two stitches: the cross-stitch and the backstitch.

Celebrations in Cross-Stitch can be used by any stitcher, from beginner to advanced. If you are a newcomer in the world of embroidery, it is best to begin with modest-sized projects. This is a real workbook. Use the designs as they are; change, add, or eliminate motifs to make your own creations, as well.

Each design is accompanied by a brief history or suggestion for its use, and, where necessary, by instructions on how to work the project.

For each design both the cutting size and the finished size have been specified, as well as what kind of background fabric was used to create the model, and how many strands of floss we stitched with. We have used DMC embroidery floss for all the projects. For each color, a number is given that indicates the actual color number you would ask for to obtain the floss. If you can not find the exact number that we used, choose a number close to ours. Since cross-stitch has become very popular, you will find that needlework stores throughout the country are now carrying linens, other even-weave fabrics, and floss.

STITCHES

CROSS-STITCH

Cross-stitch embroidery is also called counted-thread embroidery. You work with a fabric that has the same number of threads per inch in both directions—an even-weave fabric. A cross-stitch consists of two slanted stitches that cross each other. In any one piece, the top stitches should always slant the same direction. For all projects, the stitches should have even shapes (see diagrams). This is easy to achieve on even-weave fabric.

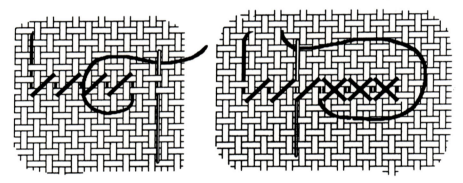

Cross-stitch done horizontally on even-weave linen.

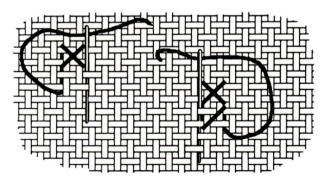

Cross-stitch done vertically on even-weave linen.

BACKSTITCH

The backstitch is usually worked in with other stitches to highlight or frame another shape or form. The stitch is worked from right to left under the fabric, and then half-way back left to right over the fabric. The backstitch covers two threads on even-weave linens, and one square on the Aida cloth. Most of the backstitches shown in this book are in gold or silver metallic thread.

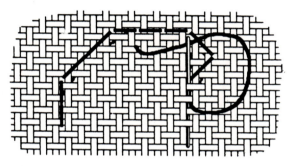

The backstitch is used to highlight a figure or shape.

WHIPSTITCH

Insert a threaded sewing needle at a right angle to the fabric edge. Over the fabric edge, overcast stitches. Space them evenly all around. This will prevent the fabric edges from fraying.

BASTING STITCH

This is a regular running stitch, which we have used for basting. The needle is worked from right to left, up and down through the fabric.

WHAT TOOLS DO YOU NEED?

All of you who embroider know how important it is to have the right tools and materials. Having them easily accessible at all times will make your life in embroidery a lot easier. Here is a list of tools that I personally have found to be of help in my work.

EMBROIDERY UNIT
Keep all your fabrics, needles, and tools in a basket or other storage unit. A portable unit is always better.

NEEDLES
This tool goes back to the early Stone Age. Then, needles were made out of bone. For cross-stitch on even-weaves, use a needle with a blunt end. If you work through a closely woven material, the needle should have a pointed end. The higher the number on the needle package, the finer—thinner—the needles. For the projects in the book, we used needles #22 and #24. Allow yourself extras. Needles always disappear somehow, somewhere.

SCISSORS
Use a heavier pair for cutting fabrics and skeins of thread, and a small, pointed pair for trimming and for ripping out those stitches that inevitably end up in the wrong place.

THIMBLE
A thimble should be round and fairly deep, and sized to fit your middle finger.

MARKER
Use a water-soluble pen for marking centers and guide lines.

RULER

A clear plastic ruler comes in handy for centering the design and outlines.

MASKING TAPE

I always tape the edges on my even-weaves, especially if the piece is to be made into a picture or hanging. Tape prevents the fabric from fraying and keeps the thread from getting caught on the edges. It also gives me some additional fabric for stretching, without having the fabric fray.

PUSHPINS OR TACKS

These should be rustproof. They come in handy after you've completed the stitching, when you are preparing your work to be mounted by stretching and pressing it (see page 17). It can be helpful to have a chart pinned up in front of you.

HOOP OR FRAME

A hoop or frame is generally not necessary when you do cross-stitch on even-weave fabrics, but some of you might be used to working with a hoop or frame, and if you find it easier, continue working the way that seems best for you. Whatever the case might be, a few hoops will always be useful.

IDEA BOOK

You will be surprised at how many good ideas cross your mind while your stitches take shape. Keep a little book nearby in which you can jot down ideas and thoughts while you work away on your cross-stitch.

MOUNTING AND FRAMING

Many of these pieces can be mounted or framed easily

with frames that are available in hardware or notion shops. For special treatments, talk with your needlework shop or a professional framer.

MIRROR-IMAGES

A few of the charts have been shown as half motifs. These have to be "mirror-imaged." This means that you simply reverse the chart from the center. If you find this hard to do, or confusing, here's a tip: Rechart the design as shown in the book on regular graph paper, using felt-tip coloring pens. The ink from the felt-tips is absorbed through the paper. When half of the design given in the book is charted, turn your graph paper over—there is your mirror image.

FABRICS

EVEN-WEAVE FABRICS

Even-weave fabrics come in a variety of widths, colors, and weaves. Even-weaves are identified by number. The lower the number, the coarser the weave of the fabric. A #12 even-weave fabric would be more coarse than a #20 even-weave fabric.

For this book we have used even-weave linens #18 and #22 (18 and 22 threads to the inch). Each cross-stitch covers two threads in each direction. Hence, a #18 weave will give you 9 stitches per inch. A #22 weave will give you 11 stitches per inch, and so on.

AIDA CLOTH

We have also used #18 Aida cloth for some projects. On the Aida cloth, the weave is a square weave. You count the squares, not the threads. Each stitch covers one square on the cloth. Like the even-weaves, Aida cloth is identified by number. A #18 Aida cloth will give 18 squares per inch. This means 18 stitches per inch, too (twice as many stitches as on the even-weave with the same number, 18). This is important to remember, since it will make a great difference in the size and number of your embroidery stitches. If you feel uncertain about what these numbers mean in terms of different fabrics, ask for help at your local needlework store. After a few projects, it will all seem quite easy to understand.

WASTE CANVAS

Sometimes you might want to embroider a design, or part of a design, onto an apron, curtain, pot holder, sheet or pillowcase, for example. Articles like these may be made of a closely woven fabric so it will be impossible to count threads. You can solve this problem by basting a kind of fabric called waste canvas onto the area where you plan to put the embroidery. Waste canvas is woven in such a way that individual threads can easily be pulled out of the fabric. Once the waste canvas is securely in place, just follow your chart, working through the waste canvas and the fabric at the same time. When the stitching is finished, dampen the waste canvas thoroughly, and pull away the threads of the canvas with a pair of tweezers. There your cross-stitched design will be. This technique makes it easy to apply cross-stitch to just about any fabric.

It has been done for ages. Before we had commercial waste canvas, stitchers used even-weaves or gauze to transfer designs onto closely woven fabric. A few projects in the book have been done with waste canvas.

When you work with waste canvas be sure to work each part of the cross-stitches by poking the needle up then down, instead of using a continuous motion. If you do not "poke stitch," the stitches tend to look uneven.

STUFFING

Several of the projects in this book call for stuffing. Use bits of quilt batting or packaged foam stuffing. After you finish the cross-stitching trim the linen to about ½ inch from the stitching all around. Use this to cut out a felt backing in a matching color. Right sides together, using the outer cross-stitches as a stitching guide, sew the backing and the stitched piece together. Leave a small opening at the bottom for a stem or to fill with stuffing. Finish it off with a decorative cord, if you wish.

THREADS

For all the projects in this book, we have used DMC six-strand cotton embroidery floss and DMC gold and silver metallic thread (40m—3.1 gr). It is obtained in a spool, and available in most needlework stores. These threads are easily available across the country, and are of very good quality. The floss separates easily. We have indicated for each project how many strands we used to stitch the model.

Naturally, you can choose threads and fabrics different from those we have chosen; just make sure that the weight of the thread is suitable for the background fabric. The stitches should give good coverage without pulling the fabric. Again, if you feel uncertain, ask for advice at your local embroidery shop.

Metallic threads are traditionally associated with ecclesiastical work, but today we use metal threads in all types of embroidery. It highlights and enriches the overall effect on many embroidery projects. There are several qualities of metal embroidery threads on the market, ranging from pure gold and silver to the synthetic types. It is advisable to use a silver or gold thread that is not wound on a silk or cotton cord as such thread is likely to tangle or unravel.

Work metal threads in short strands of not more than 14″. Pull the metal thread slightly taut as you work, making sure that the thread does not get twisted.

HOW TO START AND FINISH

When you have decided on a particular celebration project, gather together the necessary fabrics and tools. This is a good time to organize a storage place for your work (see page 10). Remember that cheap is expensive in the long run. Invest in the best materials. Your hours of devoted stitching deserve the best.

Allow adequate materials for easy finishing. I add at least 2 inches of extra fabric all around for blocking and mounting. Prepare your fabric by either whipstitching it or taping it (see pages 9 and 11 for directions). With a water-soluble pen, mark the center of the design on the fabric and indicate the actual finished size. (A few dots on each side will do.) This is to make sure that size, fabric, and chart will work together—a kind of preventive measure before you start.

Find the center of your chart. From there, start your work at the marked center of your fabric. Read the chart carefully, and double-check frequently as you progress with your stitching. Look at the photograph every once in a while. It is a lot easier to correct a mistake if it is caught early.

On some charts, you will see the word "Fill." This is to indicate that area is to be filled in with stitches. It is very clearly marked and easily understood. This has been done to make it easier for you to read the chart and to count the stitches. Working with the chart and looking at the photograph from time to time will keep your needle headed in the right direction.

Keep a few hints in mind:

- Never knot your thread.

- Fasten and secure each end of the thread by weaving it in and out of the stitches on the back of the piece.

- The thread should never be more than 18 inches long.

- Do not pull the thread tightly or work it too loosely. The stitches should lie flat and even. Try to establish an even stitch-rhythm.

- A thread can be carried from one point to another on the back, but no farther than 1 inch because the thread will then "slack."

- If the floss or thread gets twisted, untwist it by holding the fabric up letting the threaded needle hang down. It will unwind itself.

FINISHING

When the stitching is done, check your work. Make sure all ends are securely fastened and that all stitched areas are filled. Clip and trim any loose threads on the back.

Unlike needlepoint and crewel pieces, for example, work done in cross-stitch usually does not require blocking. A good pressing will do. Lay the piece face down on an ironing board pad. Stretch slightly if it is necessary to correct the shape. Press with a damp cloth. Repeat the process if necessary. Should the piece need cleaning, dip it into a mild soap solution; rinse; let dry; and press as above.

HAPPY STITCHING . . .

NEW YEAR'S CELEBRATION

OBSERVED: January 1

In 153 B.C., the Romans became the first to use January 1 as the beginning of the new year. On the first day of the new year, ancient rites were performed to abolish the past. On New Year's Day, creation metaphorically began again. Mankind could begin another time cycle with a feeling of rebirth.

New Year's Eve has always been a time of noisy celebration. In some countries, evil spirits are banished with exploding firecrackers and clashing cymbals. At the stroke of midnight, we blow party horns, beat pots and pans, and shout out "Happy New Year"—all in a festive manner, to drive out the old and welcome the new.

New Year's Day was a time to exchange gifts long before this became a Christmas tradition. Clay flasks were given as gifts by the ancient Egyptians, and eggs (an age-old symbol of fertility) were exchanged by the Persians.

Today, New Year's gatherings are a time for new hopes, promises, and successes: a new beginning to share with family and friends.

PENGUIN PLACE MATS & COASTERS

PLACE MAT:
Cut size: 17″ × 17″
Finished size: 13″ × 13″

COASTER:
Cut size: 8″ × 8″
Finished size: 4″ × 4″

#18 even-weave linen
4 yd silver metallic thread (for two sets)

Use four strands of floss.

New Year bells are a delightful way to celebrate the incoming year. If you like, work the bell motif all around the place mats, or stitch them in two rows on each side, as we did here. For these two projects, we used the bell motif from the New Year's Runner (page 22).

NEW YEAR'S RUNNER

Cut size: 12″ × 23″
Finished size: 8″ × 19″

#18 even-weave linen
4 yd each silver and gold metallic thread

Use four strands of floss.

Here is a penguin orchestra to make the festivities mirthful and elegant at the same time. You can place the runner on the dining table or use it as a hanging on the front door.

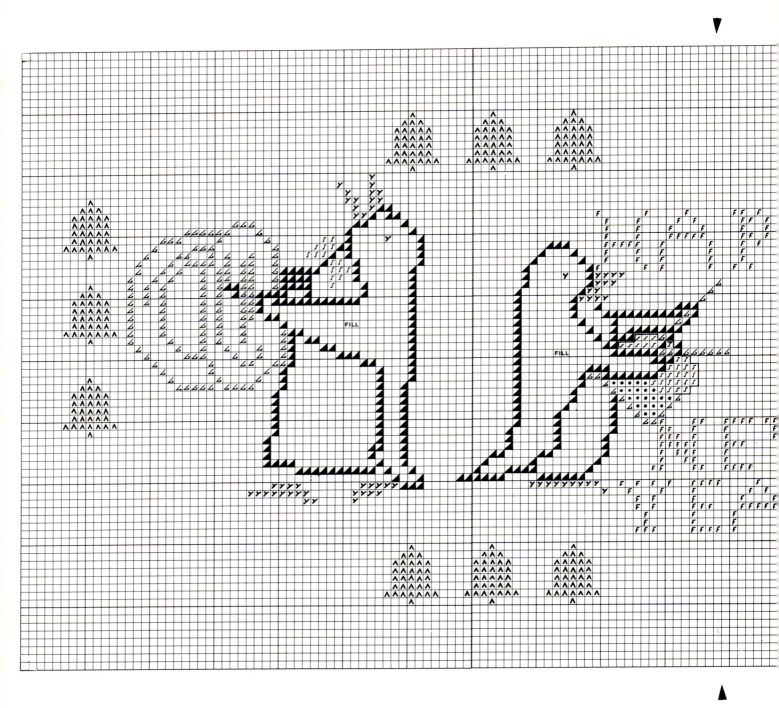

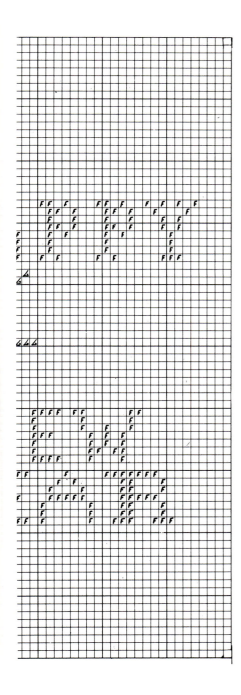

◢	Gold
S	Silver
Y	307
F	552
∧	318
•	666
◢	Black

OBSERVED: February 14

Valentine's Day is for lovers. Hearts and flowers are both shyly and boldly given as expressions of love and romance. Lovers' knots, Cupid with his bow and arrows, and sweet, old-fashioned sentiments are the order of the day.

St. Valentine is the patron saint of engaged couples, but the origin of his connection with people in love has never been satisfactorily explained. We do know that one of the first valentine poems, or "amours addresses," was sent by Charles Duc d'Orleans to his wife in 1415 A.D. The idea of sending valentines took some time to catch on. But today, "Be My Valentine" is a message everyone enjoys sending and receiving.

ROSES & HEARTS SAMPLER

Cut size: 16″ × 16″
Finished size: 12″ × 12″

#22 even-weave linen
4 yd gold metallic thread

Use two strands of floss.

Here's a happy heart for your Valentine. I worked this design on a fine linen fabric to bring out the delicate look of budding roses. This is a very versatile motif. You can stitch the complete design as you see it here, or stitch part of the pattern and use it for almost any occasion. Both the rose and the heart are beautiful motifs that can be used for celebrations throughout the year.

◿	Gold
⁒	704
Y	307
V	699
•	304

26

BOUQUET OF ROSES & TULIPS

Cut size: 6″ × 6″
Finished size: 2½″ × 2½″

#18 even-weave linen
6 yd gold metallic thread (for four flowers)

Use four strands of floss.

These colorful roses and tulips are a unique and charming way of saying "I love you." This project is easy and quick to make. After you finish the cross-stitching, back the piece with felt in a matching color. Before you stuff and close the flower, (see page 14 for directions) you may want to enclose some rose-scented potpourri. Leave a tiny opening at the bottom for a thin wooden dowel or wire stem. Finish with cord trim.

TULIPS & HEARTS PICTURE

Cut size: 16″ × 17″
Finished size: 12″ × 13″

#18 even-weave linen

Use four strands of floss.

Here are tulips from the heart for your Valentine or other special friend. This design is also suitable for other celebrations, such as a birthday or Mother's Day.

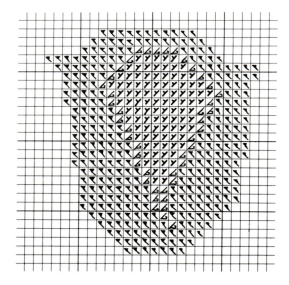

30

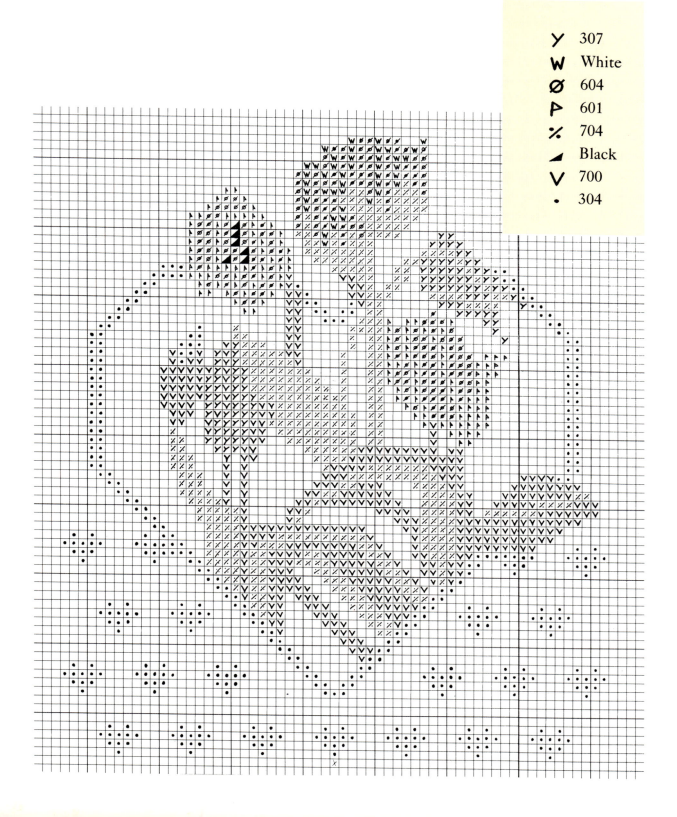

SWEET SIXTEEN

A girl's sixteenth birthday is a time to celebrate all the joys of young womanhood. The emerging feminine spirit is acknowledged by family and friends as "sweet" . . . and gifts that honor this idea are traditional.

Sweet Sixteen, for a young lady, means she is "coming into her own." It is a rite of passage that is eagerly awaited by every girl.

FLORAL-NAME BOOK COVER

Cut size: 8″ × 10″
Finished size: 4″ × 6″

#18 even-weave linen

Use four strands of floss.

Every sweet-sixteener will love a blank book in which to keep her thoughts, memories, and secret dreams. Using the alphabets in the back of this book, you can personalize the cover of a store-bought book with a name or initials. When you have finished the cross-stitching, wrap the embroidered fabric tightly around a thin, stiff cardboard. Secure the corners of the fabric on the back with a couple of basting stitches (see page 9). With household cement, glue the board with the embroidery directly onto the book cover. It's there to stay.

NATURAL BEAUTY COSMETICS CASE

Cut size: 9″ × 12″
Finished size: 5″ × 8″

#18 even-weave linen

Use four strands of floss.

You can personalize a purchased cosmetics case using the alphabets at the back of this book. Line the cosmetics case with a plastic-coated fabric, such as laminated broadcloth. This little purse can also be used for jewelry.

PARTY FAVORS—GLASS JAR BORDERS

Cut size: 6″ × 14″
Finished size: 2″ × 10″

#22 even-weave linen

Use two strands of floss.

These jars can be filled with sweets: chocolate "kisses," sugar babies, jelly beans . . . or with fragrant things, such as bath-oil beads or potpourri. Most needlework stores carry linen strips like these by the yard. They are already hemmed lengthwise. So just measure around the jar and then add an inch seam allowance for stitching the short edges together. After the stitching is complete, pin the short edges together so that the cross-stitching is to the inside and stitch ½ inch in from the raw edge. Turn right-side-out. The joining seam should be on the back of the border.

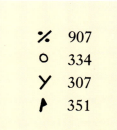

% 907
o 334
Y 307
ᛉ 351

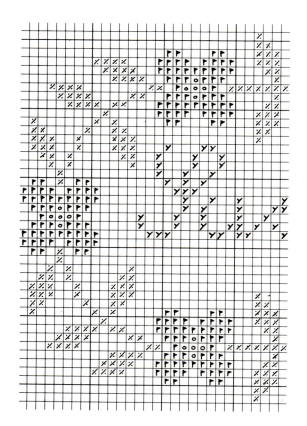

Y 726
ᛉ 3354
• 349
B 839
o 826

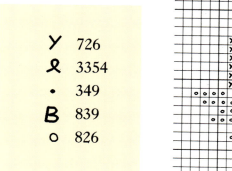

36

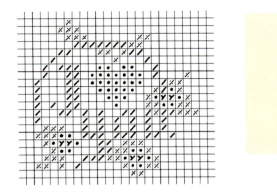

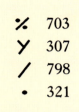

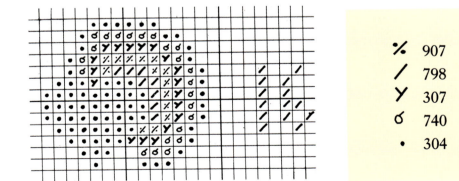

ST. PATRICK'S DAY

OBSERVED: March 17

St. Patrick's Day is full of good spirits. It's a time for the "wearing of the green" and parading—whether you're Irish or not. Green hats, carnations, banners, and streamers lift everyone's mood. Plentiful corned beef and cabbage with boiled potatoes share the table with Irish coffee and cakes decorated with shamrocks.

St. Patrick is said to have adopted the shamrock, a three-leafed clover, as a symbol of the trinity. Either the shamrock or a four-leafed clover—representing the "luck of the Irish" are often worn on St. Patrick's Day.

Today, St. Paddy's Day is a time to kick up your heels and have some fun. It's a time to be and feel as blustery as the winds of March . . .

LUCK-OF-THE-IRISH TABLECLOTH & NAPKINS

TABLECLOTH:
   Cut size: 36″ × 64″
   Finished size: 30″ × 60″

NAPKIN:
   Cut size: 13″ × 14″
   Finished size: 9″ × 10″

   #18 even-weave linen

Use four strands of floss.

Whether your St. Patrick's Day is a traditional celebration or just a good excuse for having an early-spring party . . . this handsome tablecloth will enhance the festivities. The mirror-imaged design can be viewed all around the table. The tablecloth can be made in any size.

41

PASSOVER

OBSERVED: For seven days (for Reform and Israeli Jews) or eight days (for Orthodox and Conservative Jews), beginning on the evening of the fifteenth day of the lunar month of Nissan (March–April)

Passover, or Pesach, is a time of spring renewal, thankfulness and family togetherness. The observance commemorates the flight of the Israelites out of Egypt and their redemption from slavery. It is a period of festive rituals. Matzoh is eaten instead of leavened bread, other ritual foods are prepared, and the story of the deliverance is retold in a ceremonial meal known as the *Seder*.

Passover is a time for families to relive the experience of redemption and to reconnect with age-old values that uphold freedom from tyranny and oppression. The spring holiday of Passover combines Jewish legend and heritage with a present-day need for spiritual renewal.

MATZOH COVER FOR THE SEDER TABLE

Cut size: 18″ × 18″ each
Finished size: 14″ × 14″ each

#18 even-weave linen
10 yd gold metallic thread

Use four strands of floss.

The matzoh cover for the Seder table should have three pockets—one for each of the three matzoh breads that are used during the meal. The cover, or bag, can be round or square. We made a square bag. The finished size should be about 14 inches square for each pocket. Cut four pieces for the bag (18 inches by 18 inches each). Finish all edges by hemming.

Now place the four squares on top of each other, and sew them all together. You can border the bag with lace or a fringe; it will give the bag a nice finish. We also attached three little tabs on the layers. It helps in opening the bag to the right pocket. On the front we embroidered *Pesach* ("Passover") in a sixteenth-century Hebrew lettering. The stitches at the bottom right are vowels, and should be stitched, too.

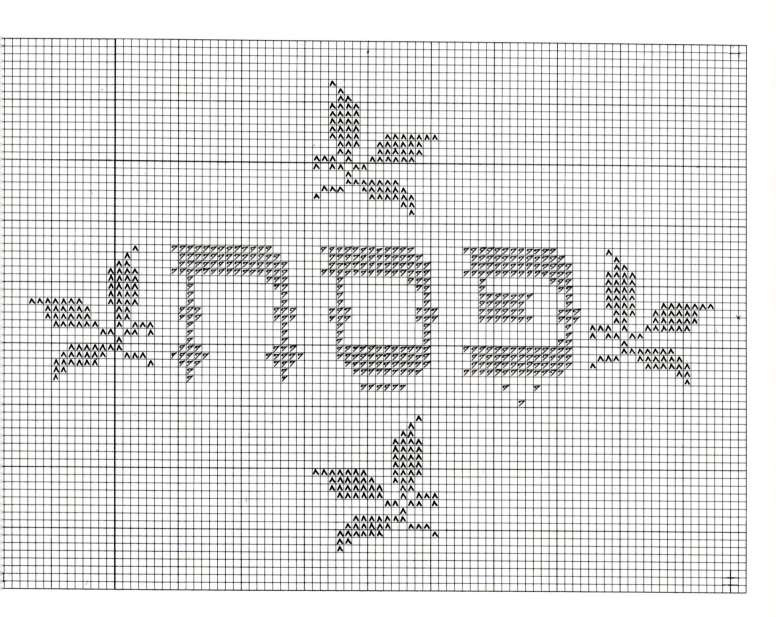

∧ 905
⅂ Gold

FIRST HOLY COMMUNION

First Holy Communion is an observance that is both solemn and joyful. Following a period of religious instruction, the child making his or her First Holy Communion receives the sacrament of Holy Eucharist.

It is a day of splendor and a bit of pomp. The boy or girl receiving First Holy Communion is the focus of attention and admiration.

COMMUNION SAMPLER

Cut size: 17″ × 17″
Finished size: 13″ × 13″

#18 even-weave linen
4 yd silver metallic thread

Use four strands of floss.

Pink and gray make this beautiful sampler simple and serene. The birds of universal peace make this a keepsake . . . and you can personalize the sampler with the date of the child's First Holy Communion.

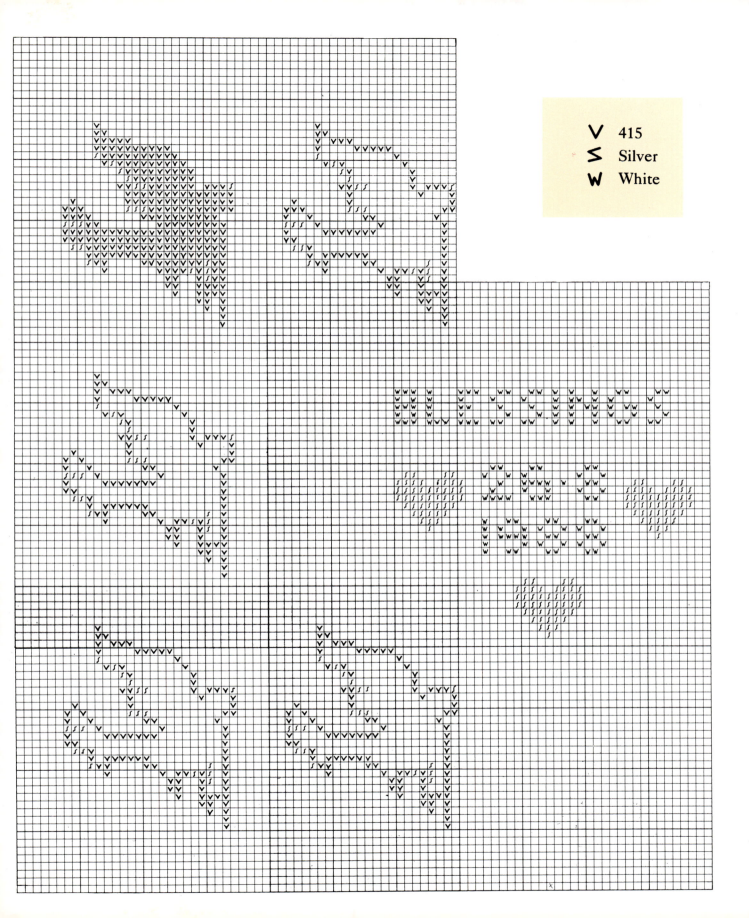

V 415
S Silver
W White

EASTER

OBSERVED: Sunday following the first full moon after the vernal equinox (sometime between March 25 and April 25)

Easter eggs, bunnies, spring bonnets, and Easter lilies are all symbols of this holiday. The feast was named "Easter" after Eostre, the Anglo-Saxon goddess of spring. The rabbit and the egg, symbols of fertility, were also associated with her.

For children, Easter baskets filled with chocolate bunnies and plenty of surprises and treats make this a very special holiday.

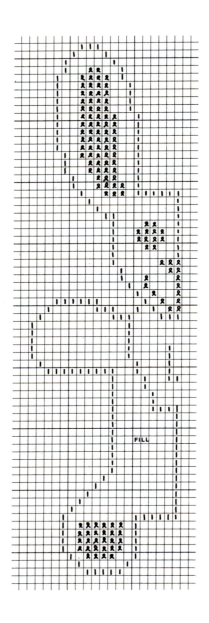

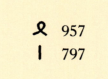

ℛ 957
I 797

STUFFED EASTER-BUNNY TOYS

Cut size: 8″ × 11″
Finished size: 4″ wide × 7″ high

#18 even-weave linen

Use four strands of floss.

Make a bunny or two for a child's Easter basket . . . or make a whole garland of bunnies for a baby. You can personalize each one with an initial. After the stitching is done, make a liner, and fill it with stuffing. (See page 14 for directions.) Finish it off with decorative cord.

EASTER-EGG RUNNER

Cut size: 14″ × 30″
Finished size: 10″ × 26″

#18 even-weave linen
2 yd silver metallic thread
16 yd gold metallic thread

Use four strands of floss.

Here is a splendid, cheerful way to celebrate Easter. The six brightly colored eggs appeal to children and grown-ups alike. You can stitch the eggs as they are shown here . . . or arrange them on the runner any way you like. You can also make stuffed eggs to place in an Easter basket. (See page 14 for directions.)

Symbol	Color	Symbol	Color
◿	Gold	I	820
•	349	◢	317
▶	550	♂	971
Y	973	Ƨ	Silver
V	701	o	794
/	792		

HEN-IN-A-BOX

Cut size: 12″ × 15″
Finished size: 8″ × 11″

#18 even-weave linen

Use four strands of floss.

This Easter hen can decorate your kitchen or dining area all year around. A wooden box frame with a bottom rim deep enough to make a shelf for small candy, Easter eggs, or jelly beans makes a handsome border.

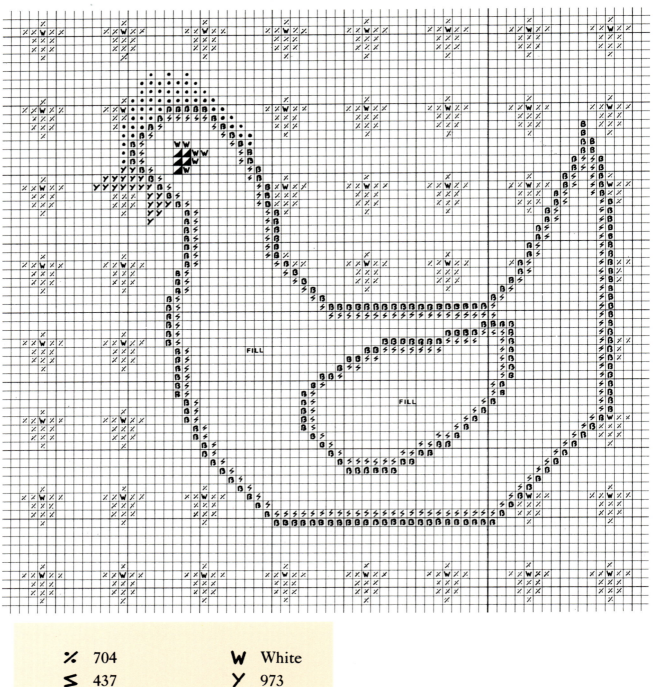

FILL

FILL

✕	704	W	White
S	437	Y	973
◢	535	•	606
B	898		

60

MOTHER'S DAY

OBSERVED: Second Sunday in May

This holiday is closely linked to ancient spring festivals dedicated to the Persian mother goddess Cybele. These celebrations honored the feminine principle of life.

The first Mother's Day was held on May 10, 1908, in West Virginia. Today the observance has become an international public expression of our love and reverence for motherhood. It's "her day," and all the family is ready to pamper Mom with breakfast in bed and smartly wrapped gifts.

Just for You on Mother

FLORAL PILLOWS—
LILY OF THE VALLEY & IRISES

LILY OF THE VALLEY:
   Cut size: 13″ × 18″
   Finished size: 9″ × 14″

   4 yd silver metallic thread

IRISES:
   Cut size: 12″ × 16″
   Finished size: 8″ × 12″

   #18 even-weave linen

Use four strands of floss.

These pillows will brighten any room by bringing in fresh spring blooms. They are a perfect, thoughtful way to show Mother that you care. These charming and unique pillow designs are also suitable for framing.

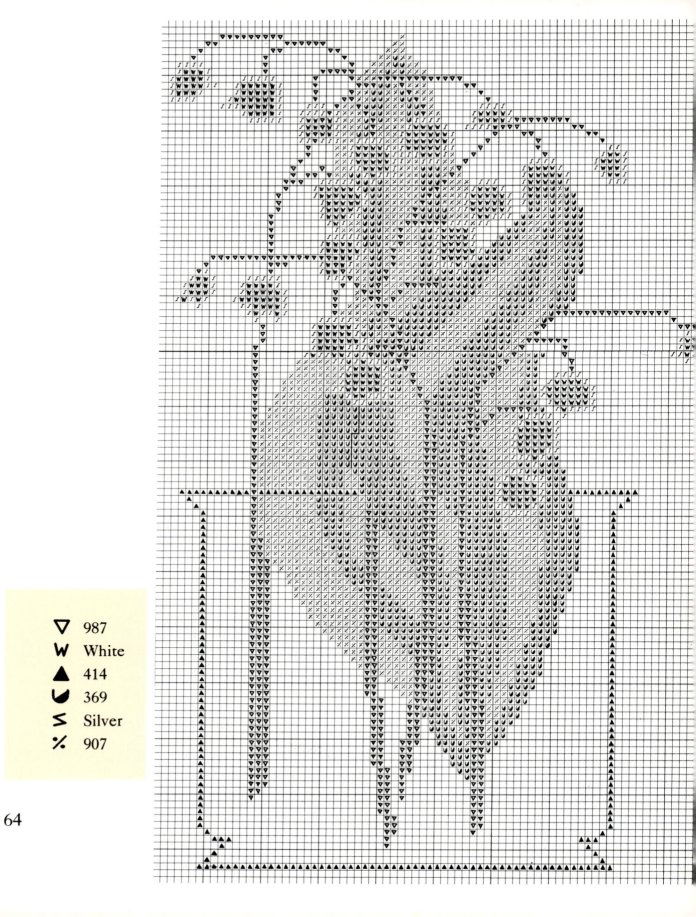

▽ 987
W White
▲ 414
U 369
S Silver
% 907

V	700
I	796
o	794
✕	704

SACHETS FOR MOM

HEART:

    Cut size: 8″ × 8″

    Finished size: 3½″ wide × 4″ high

DRAWSTRING BAG:

    Cut size: 6″ × 7″

    Finished size: 2″ × 3″

    #22 even-weave linen

Use two strands of floss.

What could be more quaint or thoughtful than an old-fashioned sachet for the drawer or closet? Gather lavendar from a garden, or get it from an herb or specialty store. This very special gift does not require much fabric, or time.

Put the lavendar into liners made in the same size fabric as your cross-stitching. The liners can be stuffed into the bag or heart. To make the bag or heart, fold your fabric in half and center the design on one-half of the fabric. After working the cross-stitches, make a heart template from cut paper to frame the flowers and guide you in trimming the edges. (The bag requires no template.) Add lace or ribbon around the heart. For the bag, do a running stitch twice around the top and then just pull the threads to close the top.

The heart, the little bag, or any other small motif, can be framed to make a charming piece of jewelry or a small memento.

⁒	704
⚑	604
o	794
Y	726
Ѱ	552

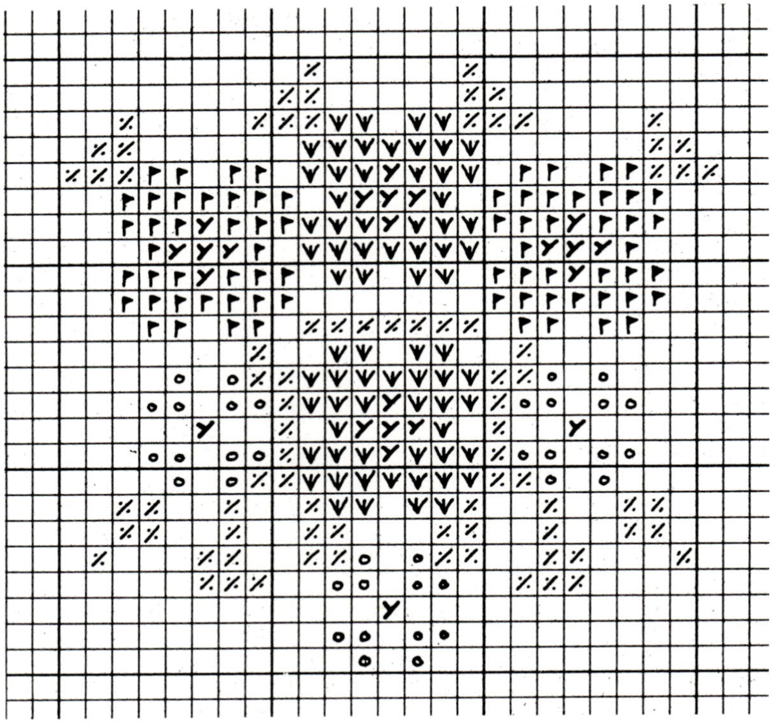

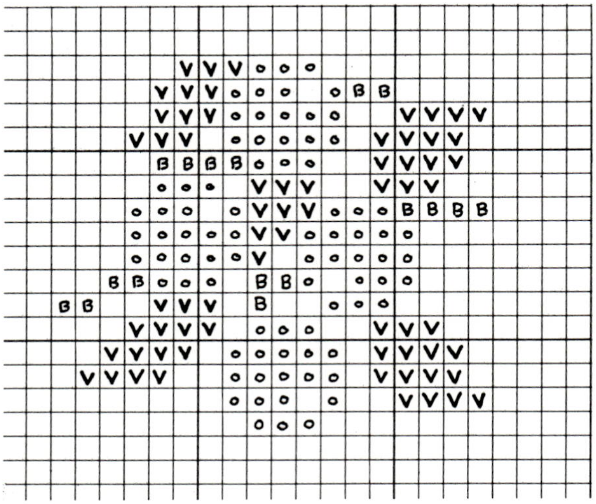

B	436
o	794
V	700

MOM'S FAVORITE SAYING

Cut size: 10″ × 14″
Finished size: 6″ × 10″

#18 even-weave linen

Use four strands of floss.

Whatever Mom's usual quip, it can be stitched by using the alphabets at the back of this book. If your mother is a dieter, a jogger, or a workaholic, she'll appreciate a funny message about her foibles. Or choose a saying that Mom uses frequently to guide her life . . . . Or just the old-fashioned "I love you, Mom." The saying used here suits a traveling Mom.

Eyelet or lace can be added to the pillow for a special feminine touch.

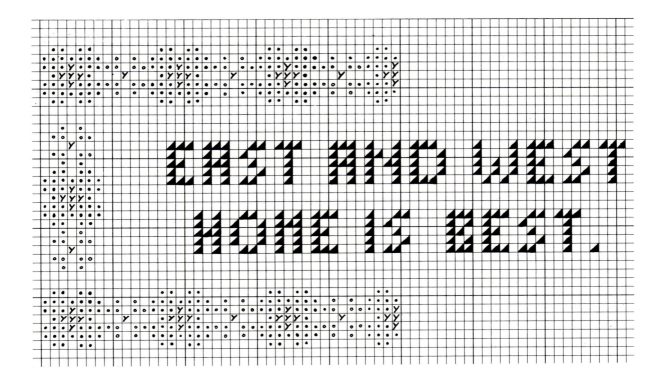

EAST AND WEST
HOME IS BEST.

FATHER'S DAY

OBSERVED: Third Sunday in June

Fathers have their special day, too. The idea of honoring fathers was first promoted in 1910. Since then, many neckties and tennis racquets have been unwrapped to the happy screeches of children and the applause of grown-ups. It's a time of pride. Often the father is the proudest of all at this happy family gathering.

BAMBOO-PATTERNED PICTURE FRAME MAT

∕	704
S	738
V	699
➤	434

Cut size: 18″ × 19″
Finished size: 14″ × 15″

#18 even-weave linen

Use four strands of floss.

Every father enjoys having photos of his family. You can choose simple portraits or candid family outings. One way you can make this Father's Day gift a very special present from a child to his or her father is by using photos of shared experiences.

DAD'S FAVORITE SAYING

Cut size: 12″ × 16″
Finished size: 8″ × 12″

#18 even-weave linen

Use four strands of floss.

F	550
X	993
o	826

Dads usually have a pithy remark or a funny phrase that they use over and over again, such as the saying shown here. For Father's Day, you can commemorate Dad's words in cross-stitch, using the alphabets at the back of this book. What better way to tell Dad how much you appreciate him!

74

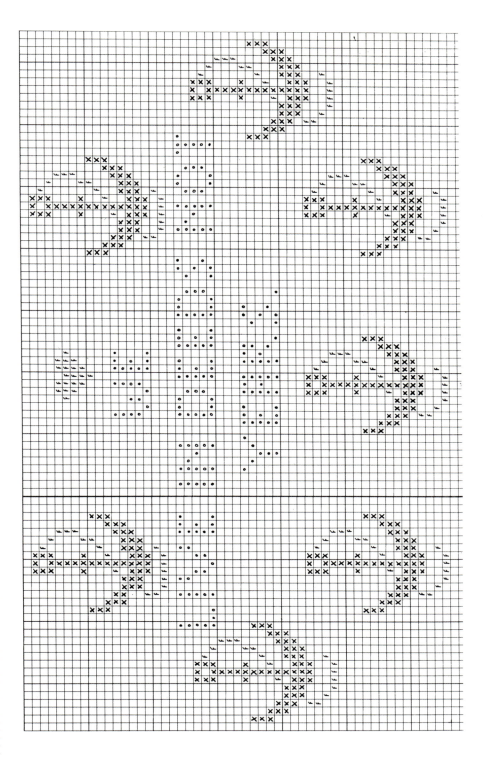

GRADUATION

Graduation celebrates both the school years and future achievements. Friends and families have always gathered to offer their congratulations and to wish the graduate the kind of good luck that lasts a lifetime.

While the graduation ceremony itself may be made up of formal speeches, the party afterwards can bring people of all ages together to commemorate the event with spontaneity and style.

SCHOOL DAYS SAMPLER

Cut size: 17″ × 20″
Finished size: 13″ × 16″

#18 even-weave linen
4 yd gold metallic thread

Use four strands of floss.

This nontraditional graduation sampler is a potpourri of extravagant and upbeat designs. You can use the motifs exactly as they are shown here . . . or you can rearrange them into your own special creation. This handsome piece will be treasured as your unique good wishes to the graduate.

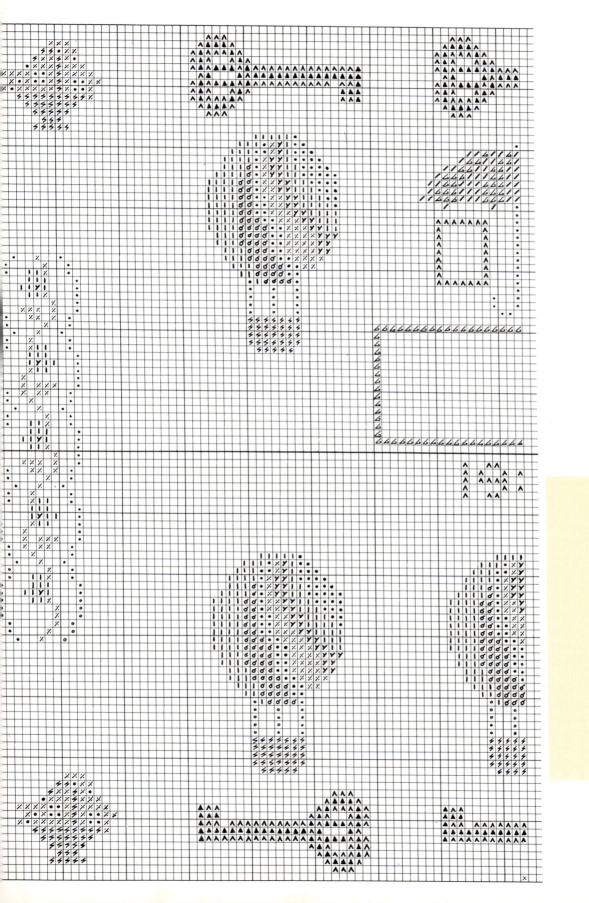

∧	762
▲	413
♂	740
Y	444
I	824
⚿	Gold
⅍	907
S	738
o	800
/	792
•	606

WEDDING

Memories of a wedding celebration last a lifetime. Traditions such as "something old, something new, something borrowed, something blue" continue to survive because they express timeless sentiments.

The "something blue" comes from an ancient tradition of having brides wear a blue ribbon on their robes to denote modesty, fidelity, and love. Rice is thrown at the bride and groom to ensure fertility and a life of plenty. And the bride carries a handkerchief . . . a bride's wedding-day tears are supposed to prevent shedding any more tears in marriage. A pretty white purse is carried by some brides, it is to collect envelopes containing gifts of money.

FOLK-ART WEDDING SAMPLER

Cut size: 17″ × 21″
Finished size: 13″ × 17″

#18 even-weave linen
4 yd gold metallic thread

Use four strands of floss.

An exquisite design in the very best folk-art tradition. Two white swans are framed by hearts with the linking symbol of two crowns. In some weddings crowns are held over the head of the bride and groom. This is to show that on their wedding day, they are king and queen. Initials and the wedding date will personalize the piece. This is an heirloom-quality sampler, and a mat with an oval opening enhances the design.

Symbol	Color
◢	Gold
I	783
/	813
Ⅴ	553
W	White
▼	320
⅍	369
o	955
Ƨ	Silver

25th WEDDING ANNIVERSARY

Wedded bliss is certainly something to celebrate—and 25 years is a wonderful milestone. It's the silver anniversary, and a time for couples to renew their commitment to each other. These days, many couples are repeating their marriage vows in a formal ceremony.

Informally, there is much talk about marriage ups and downs . . . and the love that holds everything together.

Silver is a symbol of purity and eloquence, and 25 is a number that signifies strength gained through experience. The twenty-fifth wedding anniversary gives family and friends a chance to participate in a couple's happiness.

SILVER TREE-OF-LIFE SAMPLER

Cut size: 15″ × 21″
Finished size: 11″ × 17″

#22 even-weave linen
6 yd silver metallic thread

Use two strands of floss.

Here is a beautiful way to commemorate a silver wedding anniversary. An attractive gift, it will be cherished for many years to come.

Different types and shades of silver thread can be used to add variety and create dimension. And, if you like, you can cross-stitch the leaves in color. You could also attach real linked rings to the top . . . and stitch initials and the date of the marriage on the bottom.

∧ Silver
◿ Gold

INDEPENDENCE DAY

OBSERVED: July 4

On the Fourth of July, as any schoolchild knows, we celebrate the birthday of the United States of America. On July 4, 1776, the Declaration of Independence was signed.

Today the holiday has become the epitome of the summer season: picnics and beach barbecues at which "all-American" food is heaped high on plates—everything from hotter-than-hot chili-dogs to frosty lemonade. Chocolate cookies and potato chips are crunched by the ton, and fireworks fill the air with wonder. Just about everybody loves the Fourth of July. It's a real holiday from the cares of the workaday world.

AMERICANA SAMPLER

Cut size: 14½" × 18½"
Finished size: 10½" × 14½"

#18 even-weave linen
6 yd gold metallic thread

Use four strands of floss.

This project is one of my favorites. It stands for hopes and dreams, and for the past and future. There is a place for this piece in any home—all year 'round.

/ 797
• 498
W White
△ Gold
N 434

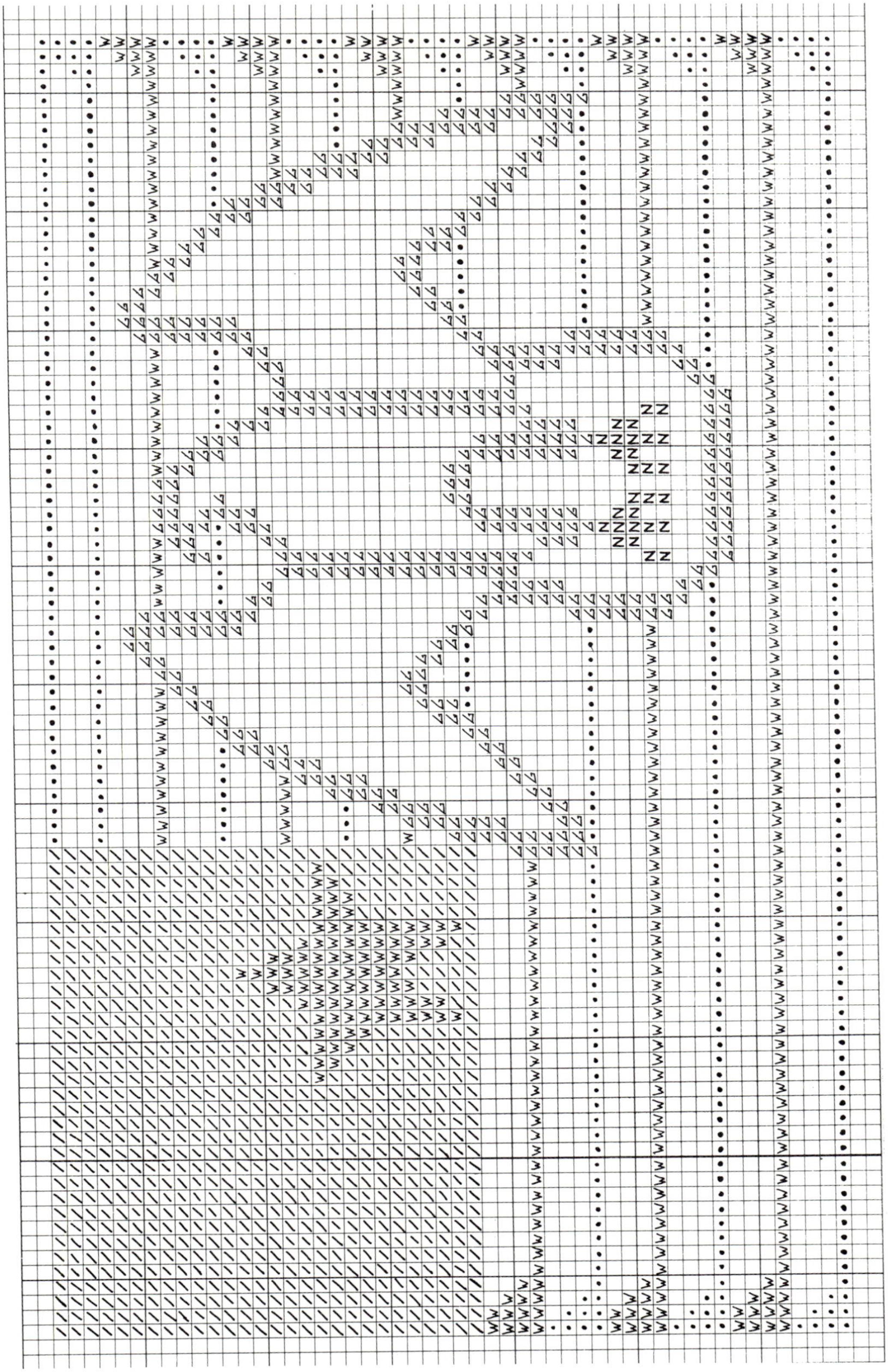

BIRTHDAY

Everyone is pleased and happy to have a birthday remembered . . . especially if the remembrance includes a luscious cake and candles. Sometimes we want to forget how old we really *are*, but then again, to celebrate a birthday brings "many more."

A birthday means gift-wrapped packages—and lots of tissue paper that holds surprises. Today birthday parties have almost become an art form, and planning inventive ways to celebrate is something that goes on throughout the year.

CAKE, CANDY & FLOWERS
BIRTHDAY HANGING

Cut size: 20″ × 24″
Finished size: 16″ × 20″

#18 even-weave linen
4 yd each gold and silver metallic thread

Use four strands of floss.

This splendid piece can be used again and again, year after year. It will make a very special day even more special. And after the candles are blown out, the hanging will be a happy memento of the event.

╱	799
✕	993
V	699
B	839
◢	Gold
✕	704
S	727
V	552
◣	310
W	White
Y	973
•	666

"FOR YOU" BOUQUET OF FLOWERS SAMPLER

Cut size: 15″ × 20″
Finished size: 11″ × 16″

#18 even-weave linen
4 yd gold metallic thread

Use four strands of floss.

What is a birthday without a bouquet of flowers? Frame them the way we did, hang them, or make them into a pillow. The bouquet can also be given on just about any occasion or celebration—or just given in friendship.

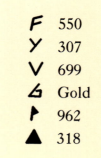

F	550
Y	307
V	699
↳	Gold
►	962
▲	318

GIFT OF LOVE PACKAGE TIES

#18 even-weave linen
1 yd each gold and silver metallic thread

Use four strands of floss.

Here are smaller versions of the Cake, Candy & Flowers
Birthday Hanging. When you have done the stitching,
fringe the material. Using a textile glue, glue the piece
onto a regular-sized business card. Punch a hole through
the corner for the ribbon.

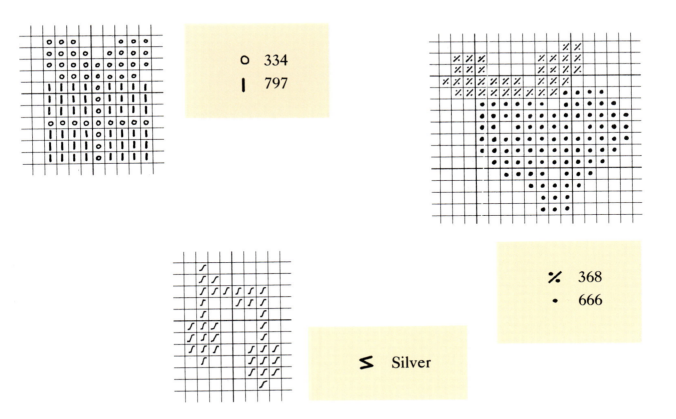

o   334

I   797

﹪   368

•   666

S   Silver

BABY SHOWER

A baby shower is a wonderful way to prepare parents-to-be for the happiness that comes with a new baby. Whether the new arrival will be the first baby or a sibling doesn't matter at all. Everyone is joyful and there is a mood of expectation.

Years ago, a baby shower was given for the mother-to-be and her women friends. These days it's becoming more and more usual for showers to be given for both parents, and both men and women are invited.

TEDDY BEAR BIRTH SAMPLER

Cut size: *26″ × 20″*
Finished size: *22″ × 16″*

#22 even-weave linen

Use two strands of floss.

A beautiful present for the new baby, this sampler is destined to be an heirloom. Stitch the birth date, baby's name, weight, astrological sign, birthstone, and flower . . . . And then hang it in the nursery for everyone to admire.

SNAKE DRAFT-STOPPER

Cut size: *8″ × 34″*
Finished size: *6″ × 32″*

#18 linen-weave linen, ¼ yard wide; scrap of red felt for tongue

Use four strands of embroidery floss (see chart for colors).

When the embroidery is completed, lay the fabric face down on a towel, cover it with a damp cloth and press. To assemble the piece, fold the embroidered fabric, right sides together, in half, lengthwise. Lightly pencil mark the shaped head and tapered tail lines. Trim off excess fabric 1″ beyond the lines. Cut out the red felt tongue and pin the forked end between fabric layers at the head end. Allowing 1″ seams, stitch the layers together around the head (catching the straight end of the tongue in the seam)

102

and the long edge line; leave the tail open. Cut a 8″ × 34″ lining piece; in the same manner as the snake, fold the lining in half, mark the lines and the seam. Turn the snake and the lining right side out. Stuff the lining firmly; turn in the raw edges and slip stitch the tapered tail closed. Insert the stuffed lining into the snake; turn in the raw edges and slip stitch the tail closed.

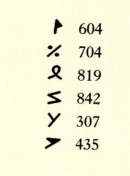

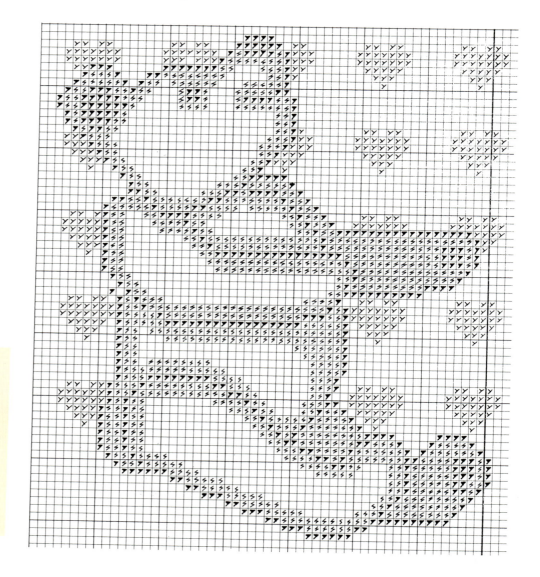

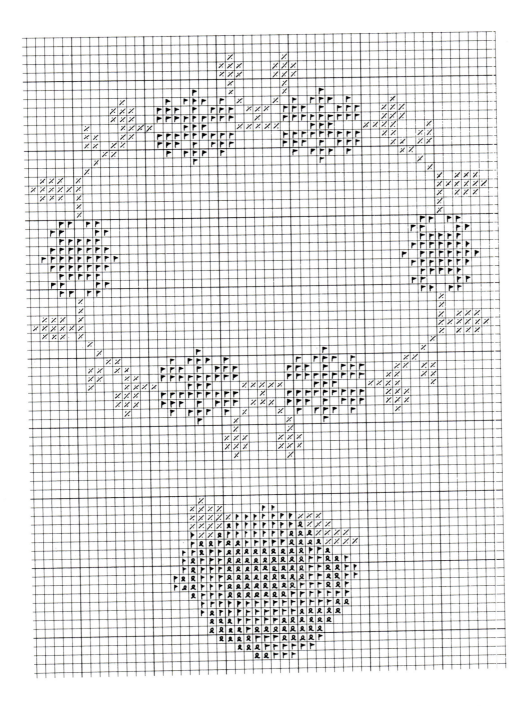

105

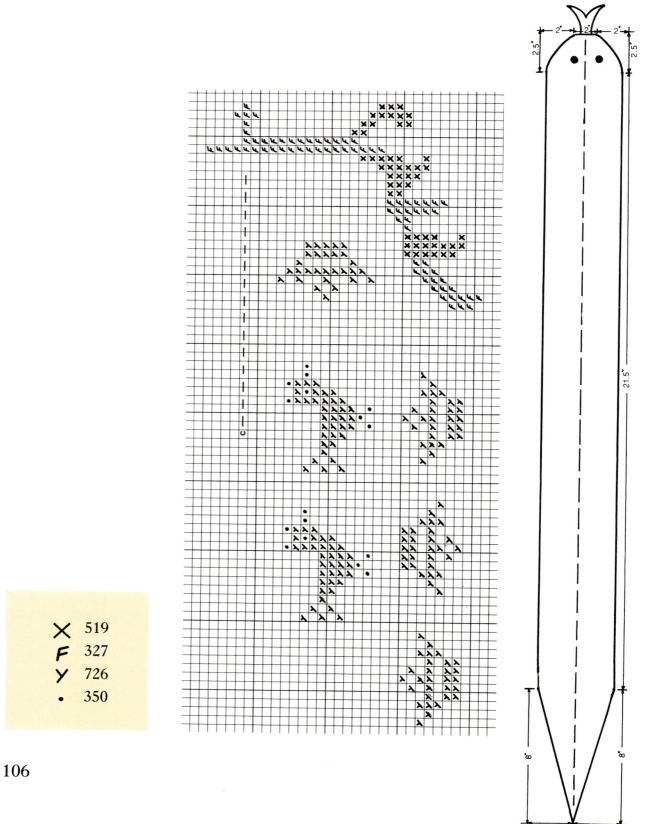

X	519
F	327
Y	726
•	350

106

STUFFED TEDDY BEAR

Cut size: 13″ × 16″
Finished size: 9″ wide × 12″ high

#18 even-weave linen

Use four strands of floss.

Babies love teddy bears. And you can personalize this one with Baby's own initial. Make a liner the same size as the teddy itself. Stuff it with a stuffing that makes the bear soft and plump. Allow ¼ inch of the fabric all around the stitches before you fold over for the backing. We backed this one in a sturdy corduroy, and edged it with a matching cotton cord. The cord and extra fabric give the bear a more definite shape. (See page 17 for stuffing and finishing directions.) And remember, you can stitch the bear in any color.

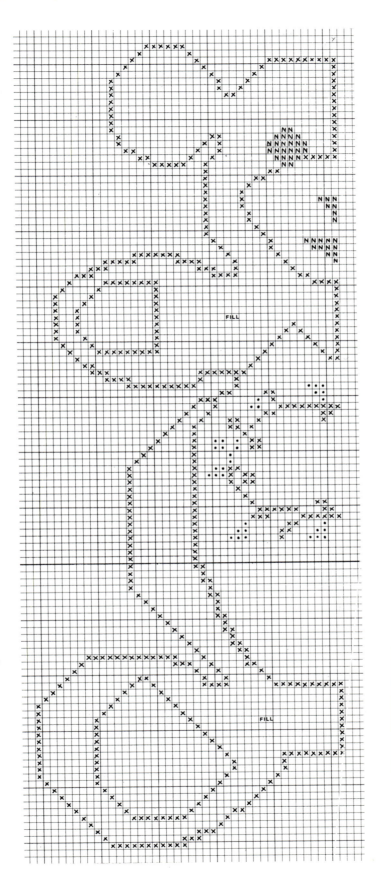

X 993
• 304
N 436

PERUVIAN FOLK BIRDS DOORKNOB COVER & PINCUSHION

DOORKNOB:

Cut size: 10″ diameter circle
Finished size: 6″ diameter circle

PINCUSHION:

Cut size: 7″ × 9″
Finished size: 3″ × 5″

#18 even-weave linen

Use four strands of floss.

These wonderful Peruvian folk birds will be a happy addition to any nursery. The doorknob cover has the shape of a small sun hat. Edge it with lace or ribbon. Make the center circle of the cover 3½ inches in diameter, and, on the back, stitch on an elastic cord to make the cover fit snugly on the doorknob. If the cover is intended for a larger doorknob, make a wider center circle.

For the pincushion, make a lining and stuff it. (See page 14 for stuffing directions.) You can personalize the pin cushion if you like.

PERUVIAN FOLK BIRDS CURTAIN

Cut size: 16″ × 54″
Finished size: 12″ × 50″

#18 even-weave linen

Use four strands of floss.

This motif matches the one used for the pincushion and doorknob cover (page 110). The curtain shown here was store-bought. You can buy very attractive ready-made curtains, scalloped or straight. If you buy a curtain fabric that is too fine to count threads on, just use waste canvas (see page 13). If you use a ready-made curtain, place the center of the motif at the center of scallops.

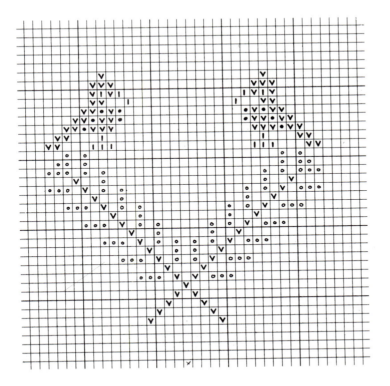

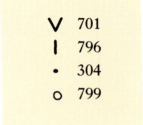

V 701
I 796
• 304
o 799

111

CHRISTENING

Baptism is an ancient ritual during which a child is blessed and united with a religious community. After the ceremony, the event is usually celebrated with an elegant brunch, and many photographs of the baby and family are taken.

Grandparents are fond participants, and everybody gets a turn to welcome Baby into the spiritual community.

"BLESS THIS CHILD" PILLOW

Cut size: 14" × 18"
Finished size: 10" × 14"

#18 even-weave linen

Use four strands of floss.

A sweet little pillow for a sweet little baby. Fun to stitch . . . and a joy to give for a baby's christening. You can stitch the child's name, the date, and the initials of the godparents. Add a meaningful personal saying, if you wish.

/ 798
o 775

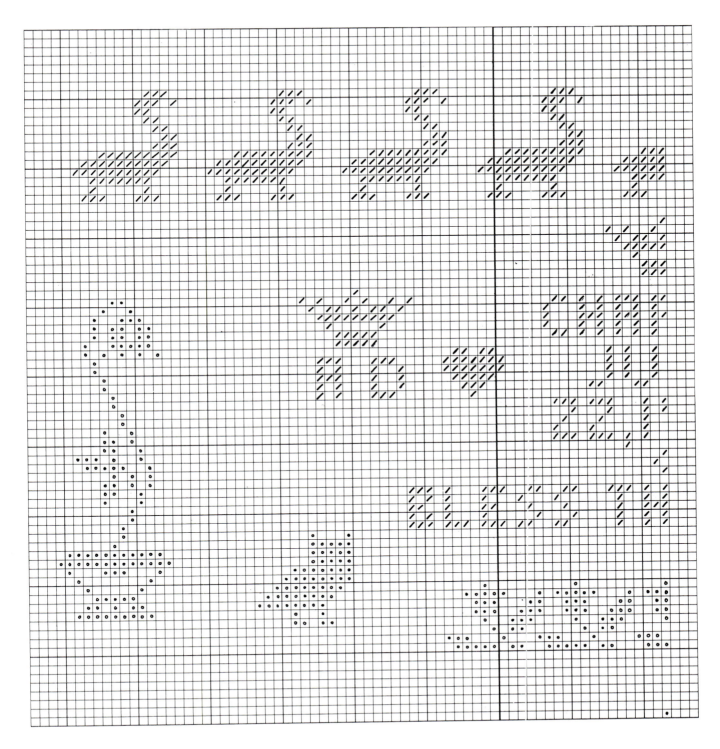

117

FIRST DAY OF SCHOOL

The first day of school is probably remembered better by the parents than by the child. It's a real "first," and one that can be documented easily by planning ahead. A few quick snapshots, outside the school or beside the school bus, will take on great sentimental meaning as the years go by.

The picture shows mementos of Abbott's days at school. The chart was made for Anna. See pages 164 through 167 for alphabets to create a photo-history for your favorite student.

PHOTOMAT

•	666
V	700
◢	Black
⁒	704

Cut size: 14″ × 18″
Finished size: 10″ × 14″

#18 even-weave linen

Use four strands of floss.

An arrangement of photos that show how your child started school—smiling or sad-faced—preserves an unforgetable memory. Place the pictures together in an arrangement that you like, and have a framer cut a mat with two openings, suitable for both photos and stitches.

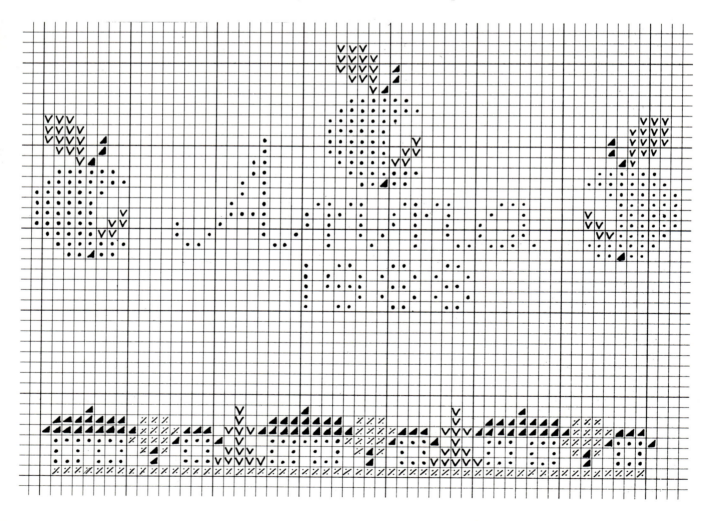

HALLOWEEN

OBSERVED: October 31

Many Halloween customs come from ancient beliefs. In Celtic lands—Ireland, Wales, Scotland, and Brittany in France—the new year began on November 1. "Trick-or-treat" is a modern version of a pagan New Year's custom. Ghosts who were thought to be lurking about in households were invited to a "treat"—a banquet-laden table. At the end of the feast, masked and costumed people paraded the "ghosts" to the outskirts of town.

The "trick" part of the custom also comes from "Mischief Night." Doorbells were rung, gates were unhinged, and powdered chalk was thrown on houses—and it was all blamed on ghosts who traveled all over the countryside on Halloween.

Today Halloween celebrations are becoming more interesting and elaborate. After the children have done the trick-or-treat rounds and have gone to bed, adults can have their own celebration. Lighting a Halloween party with jack-o'-lanterns and wearing masks and costumes is a wonderful, traditional way to celebrate.

ROUND PUMPKIN SAMPLER

Cut size: 16″ diameter circle
Finished size: 12″ diameter circle

#18 even-weave linen
4 yd gold metallic thread

Use four strands of floss.

Tricks and treats. Only the very spookiest costumes are allowed on Halloween. This charming sampler will complement the festivities. Hang it above the mulled-cider bowl, or in the entryway. Everyone will enjoy it.

FRONT DOOR HANGING

Cut size: 10″ diameter circle
Finished size: 5″ diameter circle

#18 even-weave linen

Use four strands of floss.

"Knock for treats" . . . a welcoming message for children of all ages on Halloween. You can use this hanging year after year. The round frame is store-bought. This kind of frame can be obtained in almost any needlework shop.

	Gold
♂	740
↘	783
Y	726
X	310
V	700

•	666
	Gold
♂	947
◢	Black

BAR MITZVAH OR BAT MITZVAH

This coming-of-age celebration for boys (Bar) and girls (Bat) comes after many years of studying the history, religion, and customs of the Jewish religion. The synagogue is filled with family and friends, and some of the knowledge learned is displayed for everyone's admiration. Spiritual awareness and responsibility are emphasized during the ceremony, and guests are there to give their support and encouragement.

HAPPINESS SAMPLER

Cut size: 12″ × 20″
Finished size: 8″ × 16″

#18 even-weave linen
4 yd gold metallic thread

Use four strands of floss.

Good wishes to the boy or girl on the happy occasion of
Bar Mitzvah or Bat Mitzvah. This thoughtful and special
gift aptly commemorates a very special day. The senti-
ment expressed in this lovely sampler is a wish for happiness on this day of great significance. (Turn to the section
on mirror-images, page 12, to complete the design.)

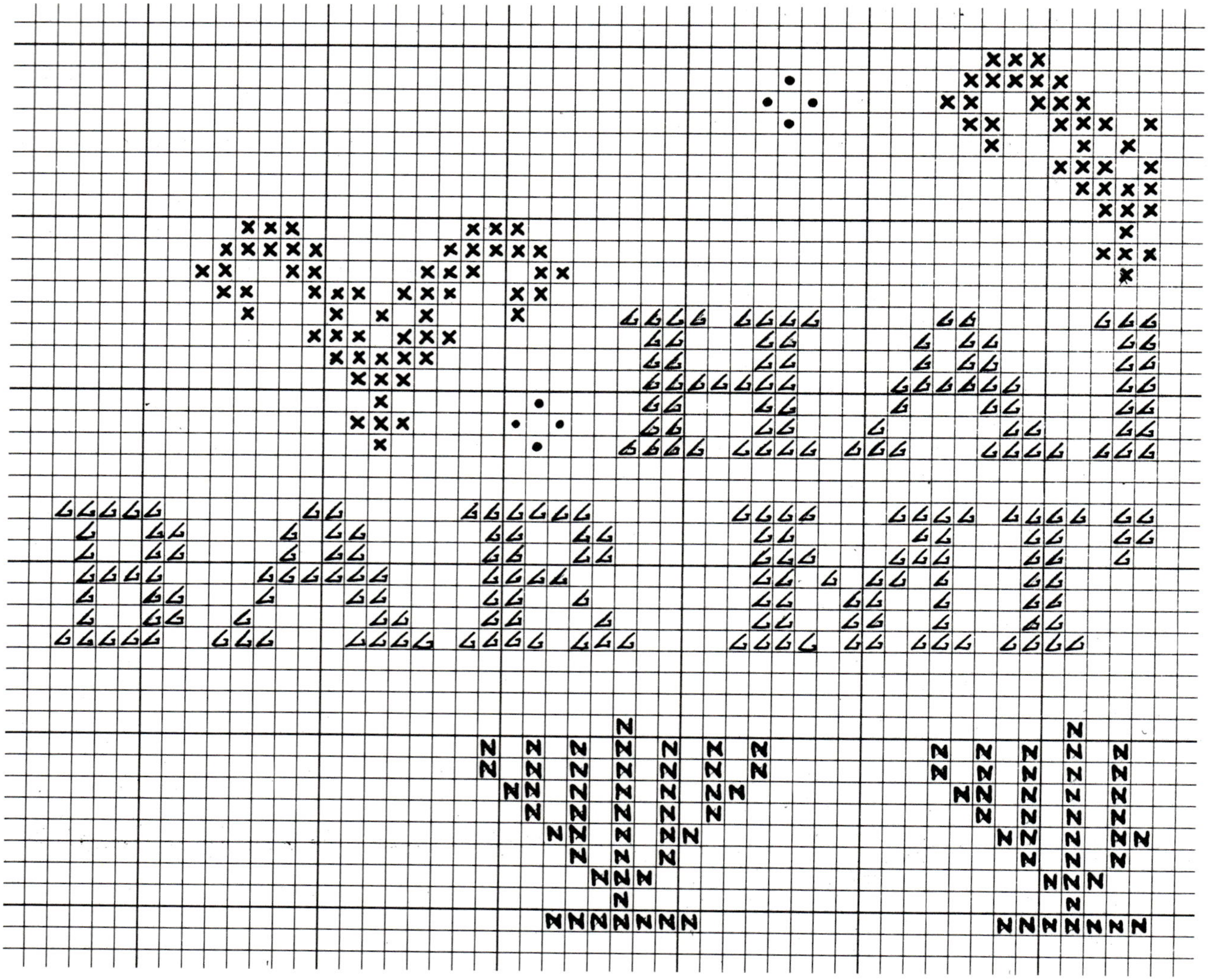

X 926
N 783
• 816
◿ Gold

THANKSGIVING

OBSERVED: Fourth Thursday in November

Thanksgiving is a harvest festival which was first celebrated in 1621 in Plymouth, Massachusetts. It is not actually known whether turkeys were eaten on that day, but we do know that the festival lasted for three days, and the food was abundant. Venison, duck, goose, seafood, and eels were among the things that were served. A very strong, sweet wine made from wild grapes was a flavorful accompaniment.

Today Thanksgiving still means feasting sumptuously and giving thanks for the bounty that is available to us. And there are parades and football games that remind us that Christmas is not far away.

HARVEST SAMPLER

Cut size: 17″ × 17″
Finished size: 13″ × 13″

#18 even-weave linen

Use four strands of floss.

Pumpkin, corn, squash, and corn husk . . . . The colors of fall and of the harvest abound on this striking piece. The harvest sampler brings all the best of Thanksgiving season into your home. Make this project for yourself or as a holiday gift.

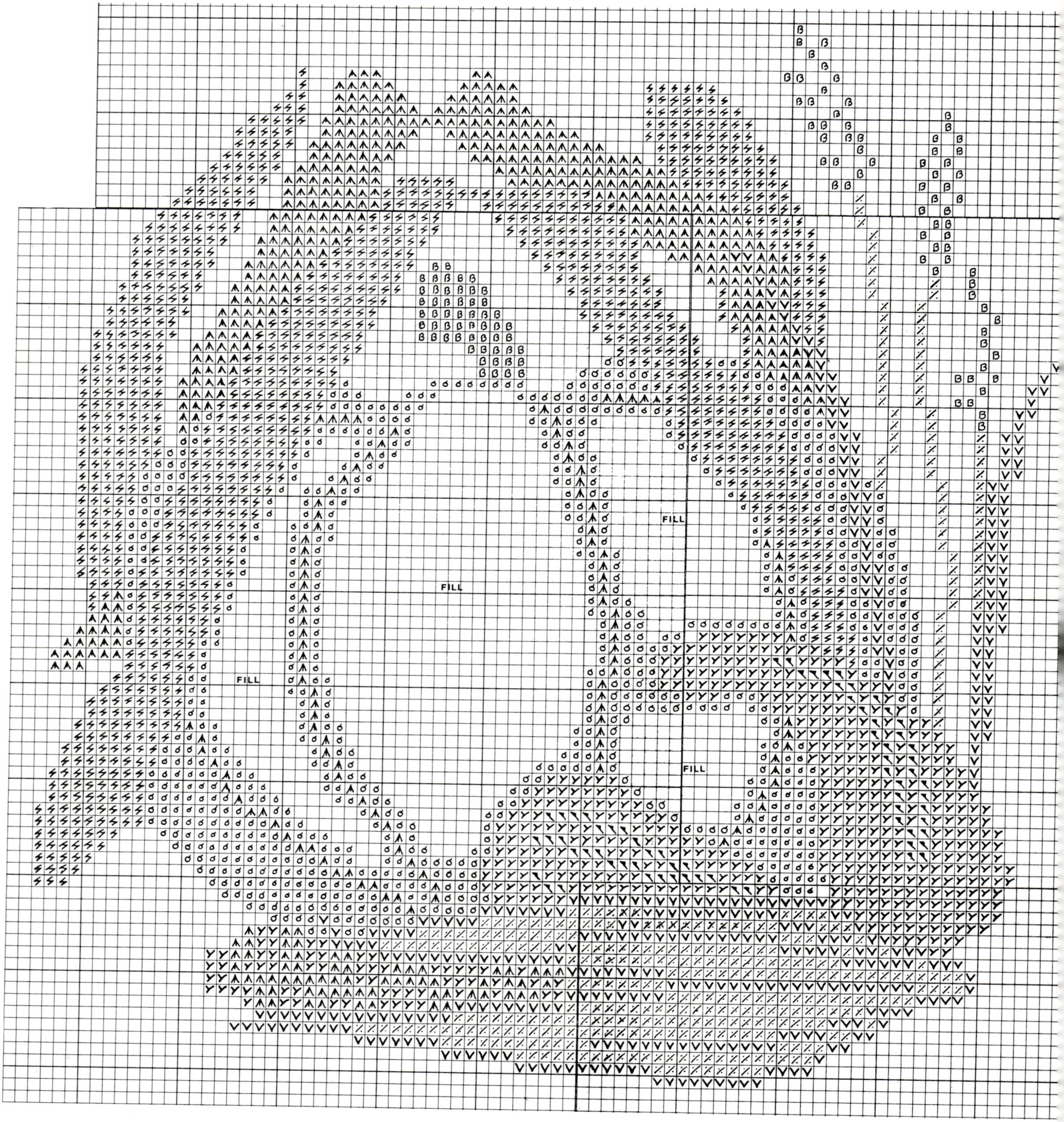
FILL
FILL
FILL
FILL

NATURE'S BOUNTY RUNNER
& NAPKINS

RUNNER:

    Cut size: 18″ × 34″

    Finished size: 14″ × 30″

NAPKIN:

    Cut size: 13″ × 14″

    Finished size: 9″ × 10″

    #18 even-weave linen

Use four strands of floss.

Decorate the Thanksgiving table with this lovely runner, which will be treasured for many holidays to come. This runner can easily be extended to fit any table size. The border design (charted on page 156) may be picked up in the napkins.

⊆	436
∧	739
⁒	472
B	838
♂	971
⊾	727
V	469
Y	307

An Invitation

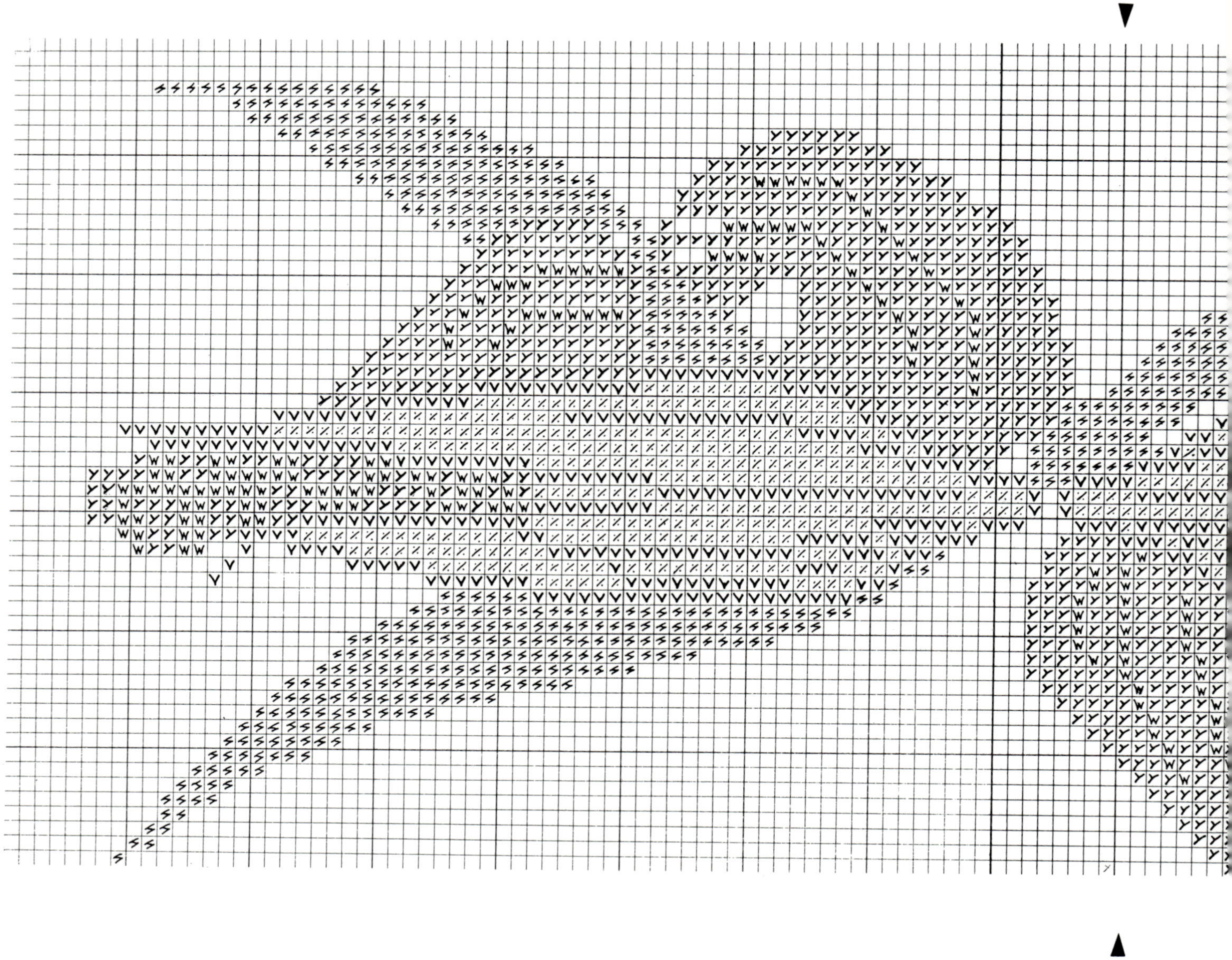

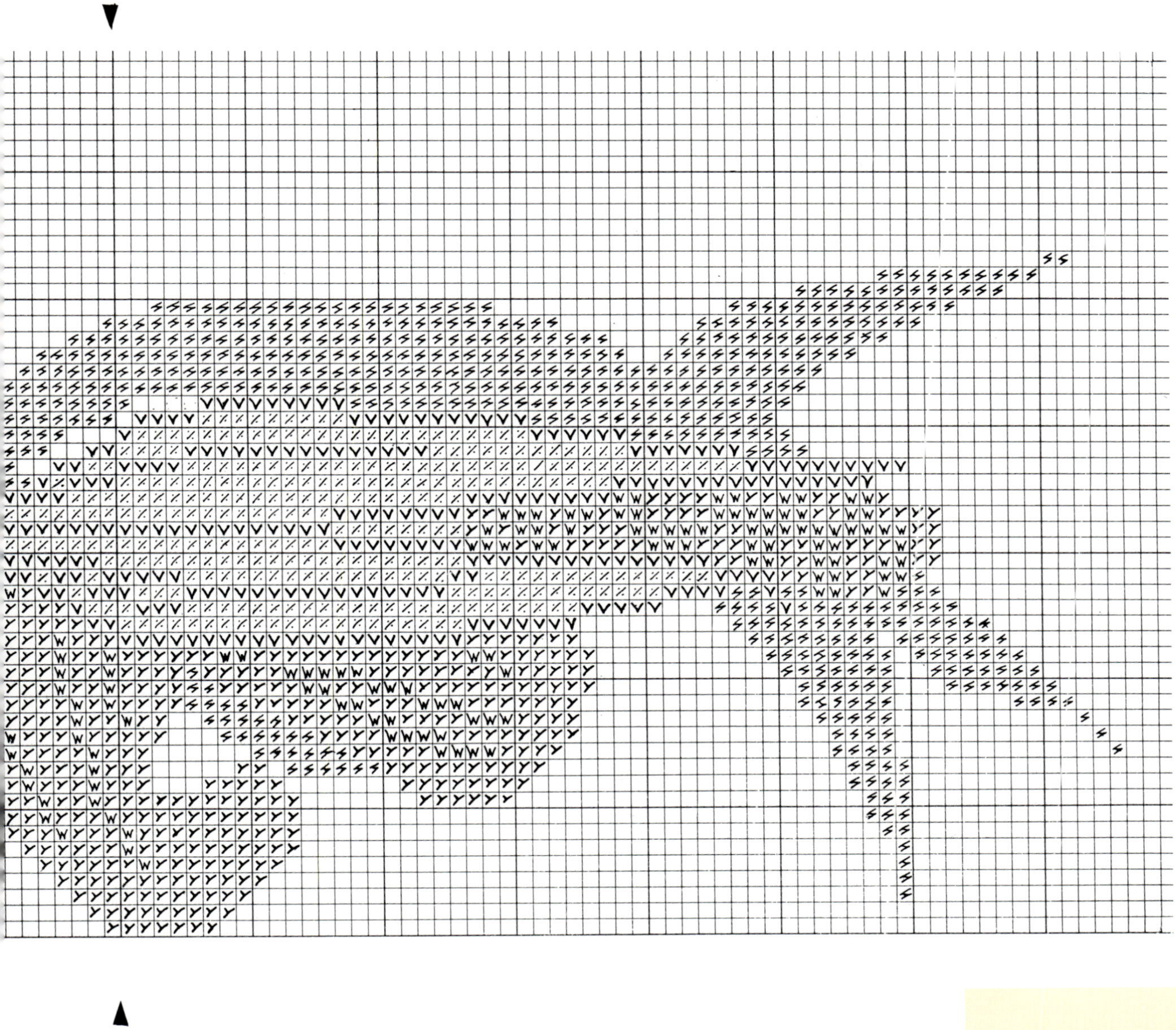

Y	743
V	469
W	712
≤	841
%	907

HANUKKAH

OBSERVED: For eight days beginning on the twenty-fifth day of the lunar month of Kislev (November–December)

Hanukkah—the Festival of Lights—is a religious celebration. Candles are lighted each night for eight nights. The usual practice is to add a light each night until all are lit. The custom is explained by a Talmudic legend that says when the Maccabees wanted to rekindle the sacred lamp in the temple, they found oil to last only one day. But by a miracle it burned for eight days.

During Hanukkah, gifts are exchanged and traditional festive meals are prepared. Children play with four-sided tops called dreidels. Each side is marked with a Hebrew letter: *N, G, H,* or *S.* It is said that these letters stand for the Hebrew motto "Nes Gadol Hayah Sham"—"A Great Miracle Happened Here."

MENORAH SAMPLER

Cut size: 15″ × 17″ oval
Finished size: 11″ × 13″ oval

#18 even-weave linen
4 yd each gold and silver metallic thread

Use four strands of floss.

This is an ancient version, patterned after the menorah in Solomon's Temple. It is similar to the nine-branched menorah used to celebrate Hanukkah, but this one has seven branches which symbolize the seven days of the Creation. This is an emblem for the State of Israel.

The sampler is simple and elegant, and it can be a beautiful decoration for your home all year around.

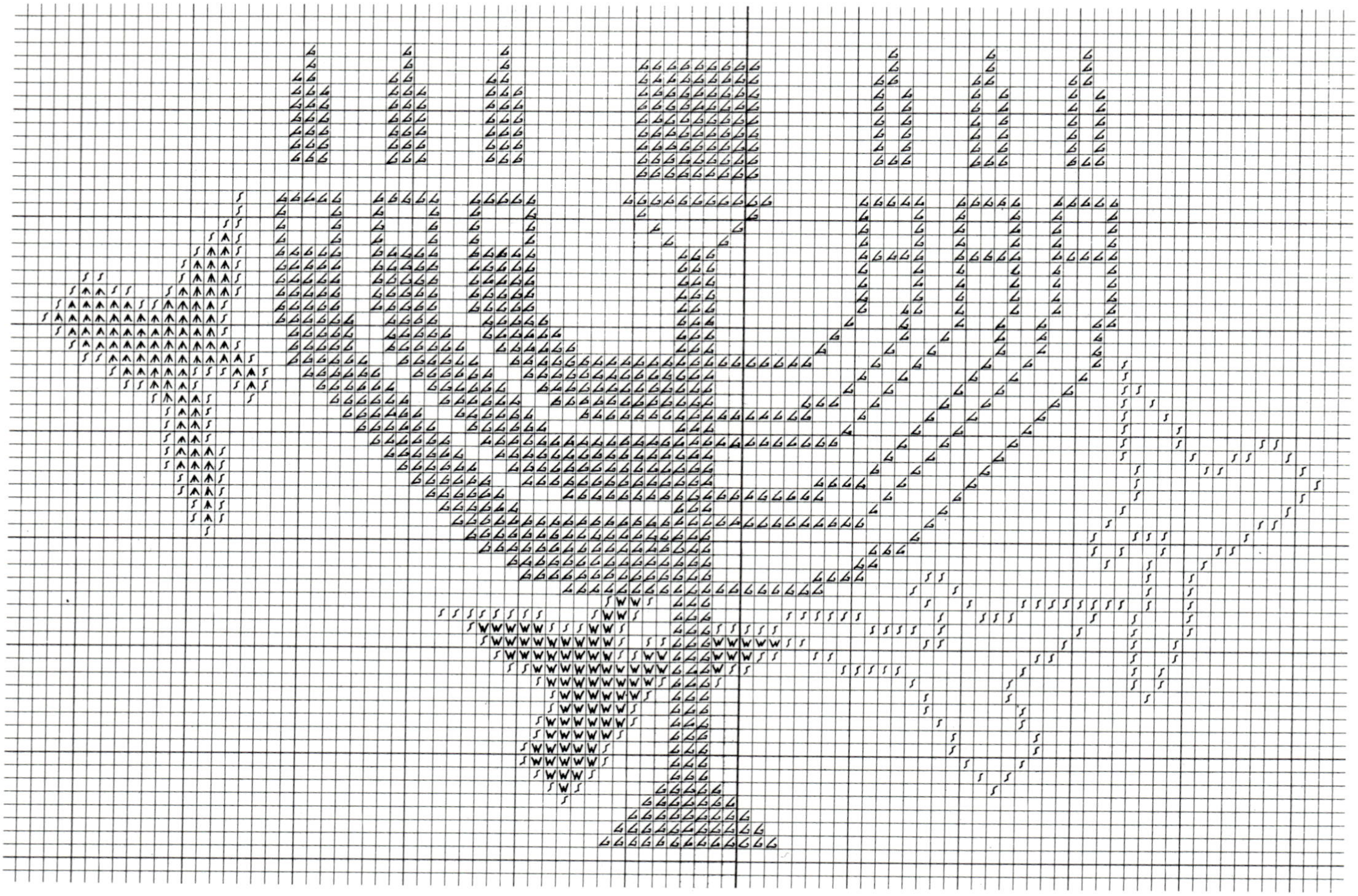

△ Gold
S Silver
∧ 712
W White

CHRISTMAS

OBSERVED: December 25

Radiant Christmas candles and the burning of the Yule log; mistletoe, holly, poinsettia plants, and a fir tree; the crèche; gift-giving and carol singing—all are ways we commemorate the birth of Christ. Holiday cheer is the essential ingredient for a merry Christmas. In today's world, the Christmas spirit means leaving the cares of winter behind and joining with family and friends for a time of renewal.

Christmas is steeped in tradition. Sending cards began in England in the 1840s. One of the first representations of a decorated Christmas tree showed playful Victorian children dancing around it.

The Germans are credited with introducing the Christmas tree into the holiday celebration. And in this country, the first Christmas tree, as legend has it, was introduced by August Imgard, a 21-year-old immigrant from Bavaria.

SANTA SAMPLER

Cut size: 18″ × 20″
Finished size: 14″ × 16″ (loops not included)

#18 even-weave linen
4 yd gold metallic thread

Use four strands of floss.

Ho, ho, ho! This is a merry, welcoming hanging. Or you can frame it . . . or make a big pillow. Jolly—and anywhere you place it, it will make the whole room festive. A wonderful, wonderful gift, or make it for your own next Christmas celebration.

V	700
•	666
/	793
⊊	738
B	838
◿	Gold
◀	727
Λ	762

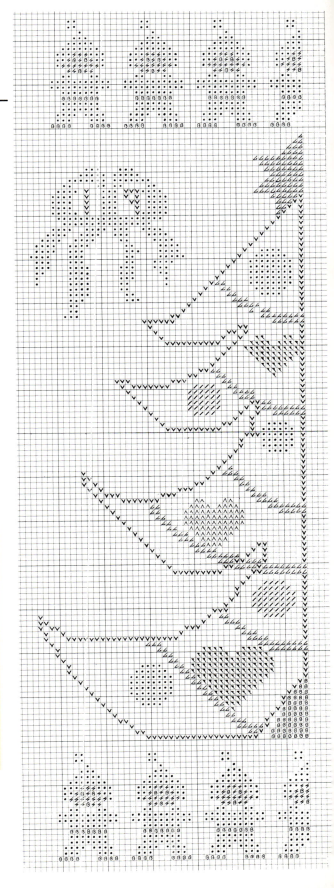

SANTA & BEADED ANGEL DOLLS

SANTA:

    Cut size: 8″ × 10″

    Finished size: 4″ high × 6″ wide

ANGELS:

    Cut size: 8″ × 9″

    Finished size: 4″ × 5″

    #18 even-weave linen

    3 yd each gold and silver metallic thread

    Beads (for angels)

Use four strands of floss.

Here're Santa and two adorable beaded angels. The Santa is stylized and can also be made as a hanging, a framed picture, or a pillow. Because of his geometry, he is easy to enlarge. We backed Santa and the angels with felt, made liners, filled them with stuffing, and finished the edges with cord (which also formed the loops for hanging Santa and the angels).

HOLIDAY GIFT TAGS

    #18 even-weave linen

    1 yd each gold and silver metallic thread

Use four strands of floss.

These handsome gift tags are an especially attractive way to give presents. A handmade touch is always welcome, and in exchanging gifts, here is a chance to add a little extra.

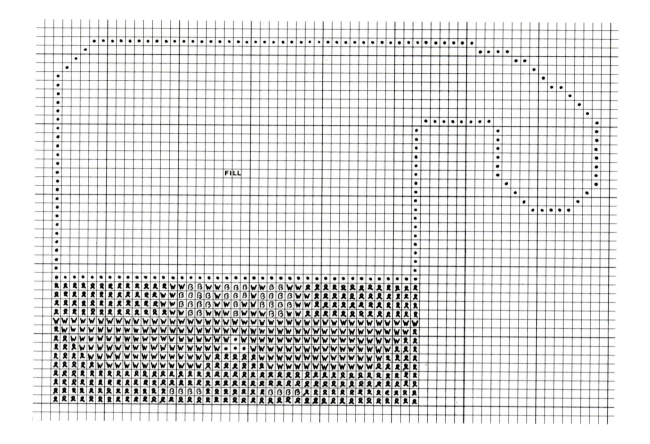

FILL

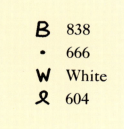

B   838
•   666
W   White
ℛ   604

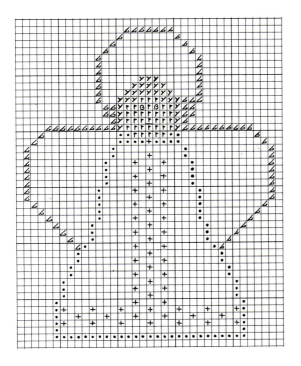

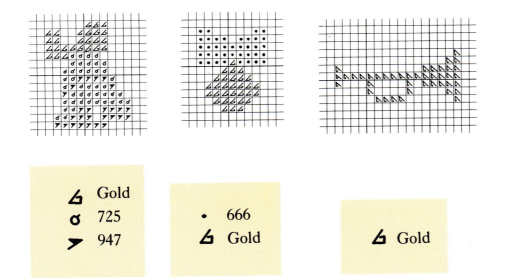

⌔ Gold
Y 307
• 666
B 838
+ Beads

⌔ Gold
♂ 725
➤ 947

• 666
⌔ Gold

⌔ Gold

REINDEER POT HOLDERS
& APRON SET

Waste canvas

Use two strands of floss.

The reindeer is a charming and well-known holiday motif that everyone loves. Both the apron and the pot holders are store-bought. The design is applied through waste canvas (see page 13).

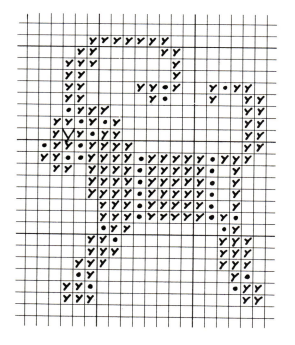

Y 307
• 666

CHRISTMAS HEARTS PLACE MATS & NAPKIN RINGS

PLACE MAT:
   Cut size: 17″ × 20″
   Finished size: 13″ × 16″

NAPKIN RING:
   Cut size: 4½″ × 8″
   Finished size: 2″ wide × 6″ around

#18 even-weave linen
4 yd gold metallic thread

Use four strands of floss.

A gift for the table is always a hit. And these will make bright and cheery additions to any room, no matter what the decor. They are quick and easy to make.

Hem the edges of the place mat or napkin ring neatly by hand. Cross-stitch the napkin rings with the motif centered on the ring. Fold the sides back, and stitch together (the joining seam on the back will then end up in the center). Join the ends and form the ring. The ring could be made smaller (about 5 inches around) for paper napkins.

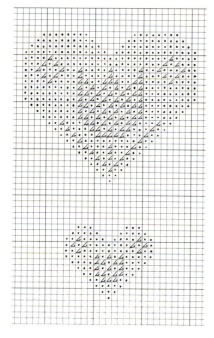

△ Gold
•   666

150

HOUSEWARMING

Whether you've just moved into a new home, or have been settled in for many years, any season is the right one for an open house. An invitation that reads "Housewarming 1-5 P.M." is an invitation to relax and enjoy the pleasure of friendship.

Good company and delicious food and drink are the main ingredients for success. Gifts will certainly be welcome, especially if they are beautiful and functional. They are a delight to create and give; a happy surprise to receive and cherish.

Housewarming means just that—a house filled with the warmth of people you care about.

BANANA & PEAR GUEST TOWELS

Waste canvas

Use four strands of floss.

A gift of cross-stitched guest towels will be appreciated and treasured. The towels are store-bought, and we applied the designs through waste canvas (see page 13).

SWEET CHERRIES PLACE MATS & NAPKIN RINGS

PLACE MAT:
Cut size: 17″ × 20″
Finished size: 13″ × 16″

NAPKIN RING:
Cut size: 4½″ × 8″
Finished size: 2″ wide × 6″ around

#18 even-weave linen

Use four strands of floss.

Sweet cherries are perfect for a housewarming celebration—or for any festive celebration. For finishing details, see Christmas Hearts Place Mats & Napkin Rings, page 150.

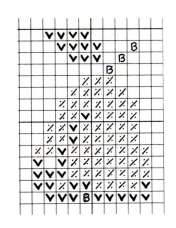

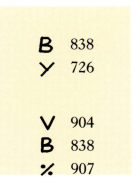

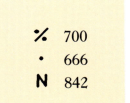

HORSESHOE PILLOW

⸓	704
F	550
V	553
◿	317
Λ	415
•	605
I	469
◢	413

Cut size: 14″ × 16″
Finished size: 10″ × 12″

#18 even-weave linen

Use four strands of floss.

Here's a good-luck motif to wish all householders well. Beautiful and subtle colors combine in this striking piece, which will appeal to a broad range of tastes.

There are many events in each year that deserve special notice. The practice of sending greeting cards to celebrate these occasions is universal. A small surprise, that arrives in the mail, or is delivered by hand to a special friend, indicates that you remembered—and that you care.

What could be more personal, or more of a warm remembrance than a lovingly stitched card. It brings a message of thoughtfulness.

158

ALL-OCCASIONS GREETING CARDS

#18 Aida cloth, *or* #18 even-weave linen
1 yd each gold and silver metallic thread

For #18 Aida cloth, use two strands of floss.
For #18 even-weave linen, use four strands of floss.

Eleven cards . . . for many occasions. These small and lovely works of art are quick and easy. We've made one of each.

Thank-You Note Card
Mother's Day Card
Jewish New Year Card
Birthday Card
Valentine's Day Card
New Baby Card
Christmas Card
Invitation (Congratulations) Card
Birth Announcement Card
Father's Day Card
Wedding Card

Buy the cards in your local needlework store. They come prepackaged with envelope and threads.

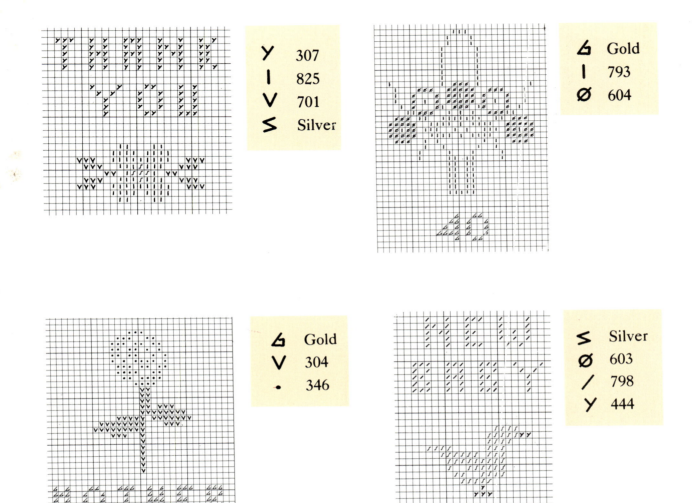

Y — 307
I — 825
V — 701
S — Silver

⌒ — Gold
I — 793
Ø — 604

⌒ — Gold
V — 304
• — 346

S — Silver
Ø — 603
/ — 798
Y — 444

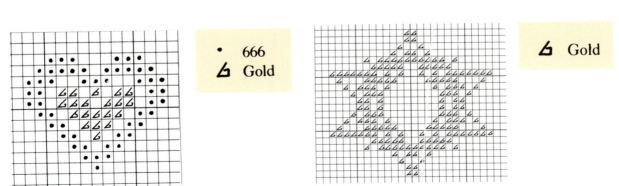

• — 666
⌒ — Gold

⌒ — Gold

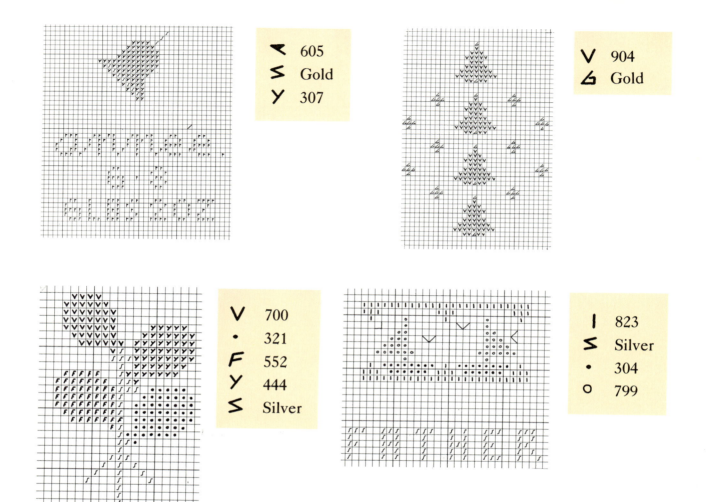

▼	605
S	Gold
Y	307

| V | 904 |
| ◿ | Gold |

V	700
•	321
F	552
Y	444
S	Silver

I	823
S	Silver
•	304
o	799

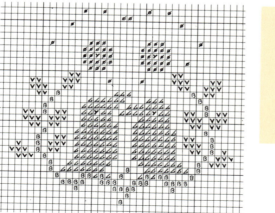

B	783
◿	Gold
Ø	893
V	989
Y	444

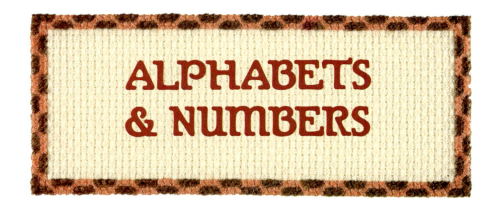

ALPHABETS & NUMBERS

Here are complete charts of all the letters and numbers used with projects in the book. Make your own choice of color for each project.

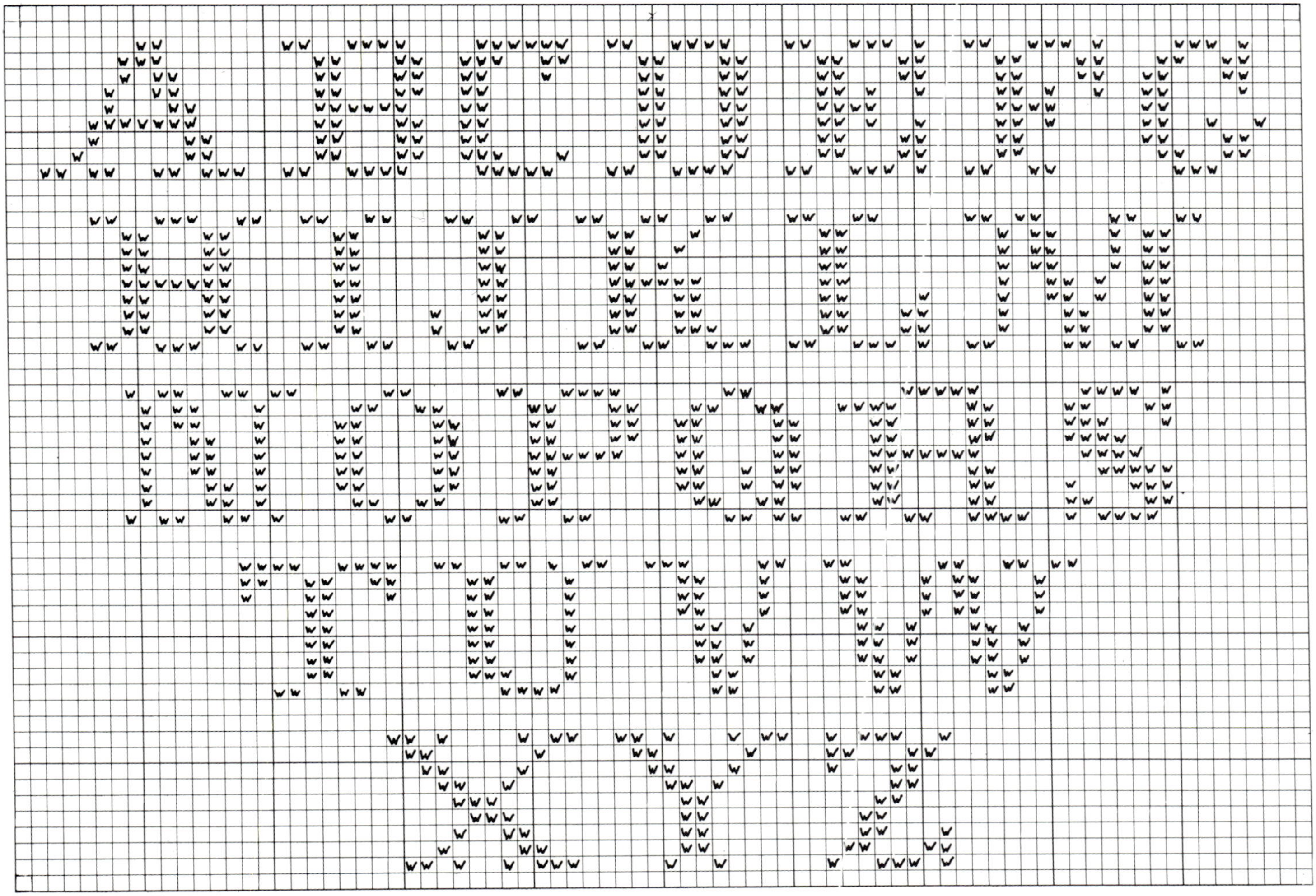

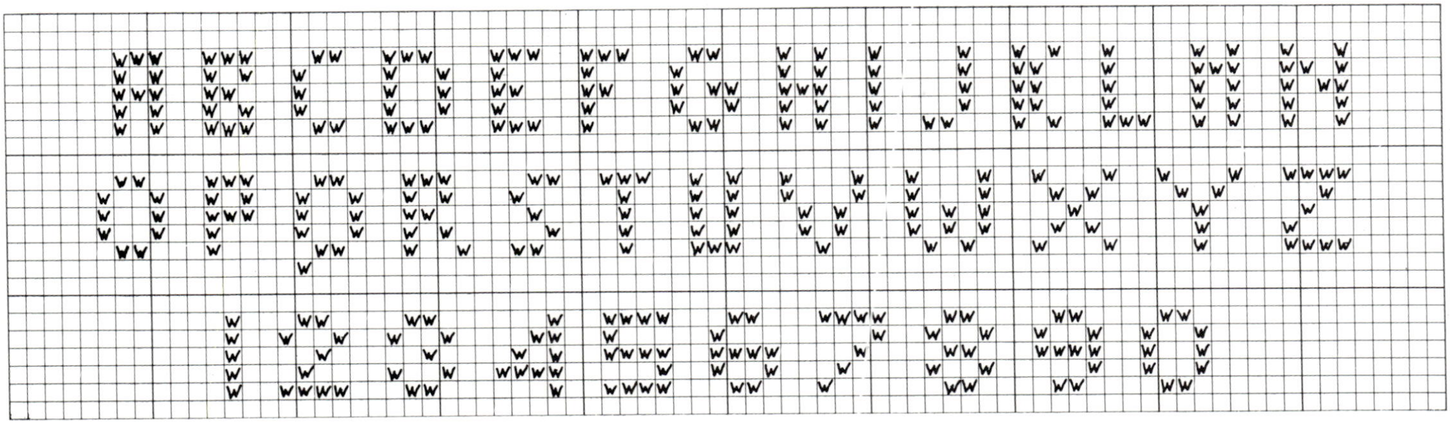

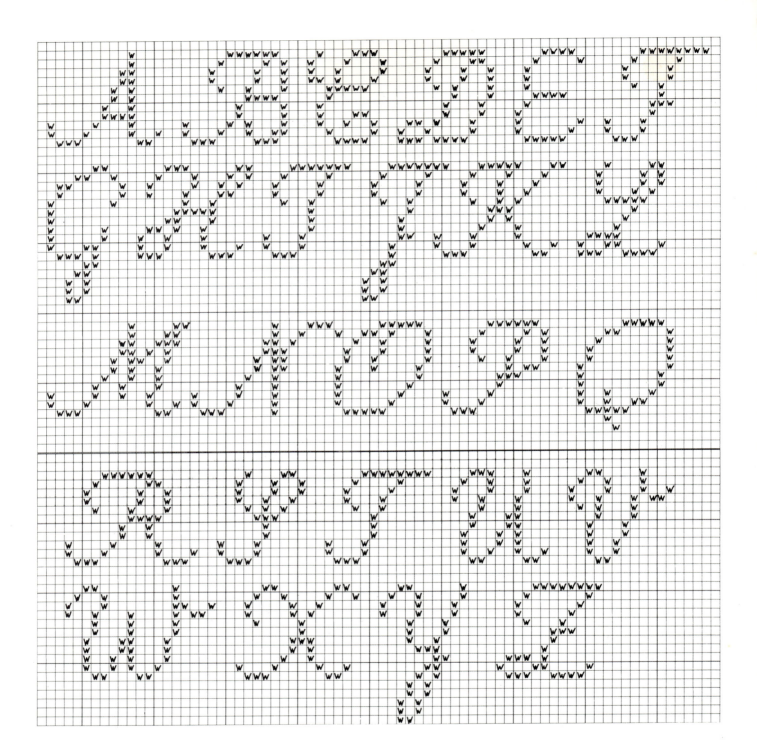

166

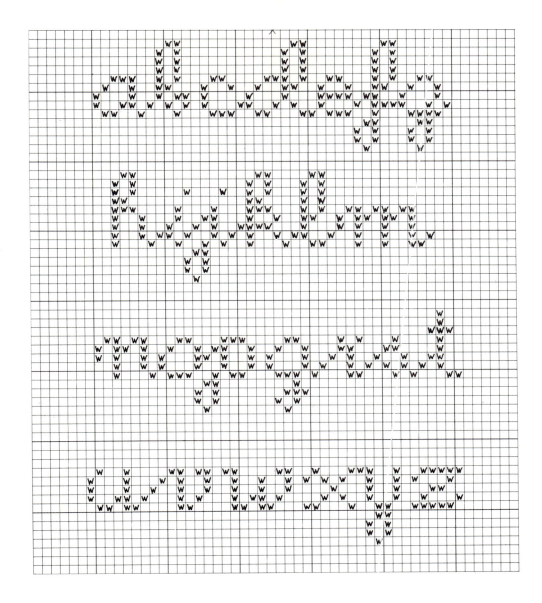

INDEX

For information on how you can have
BETTER HOMES AND GARDENS
delivered to your door, write to:
Mr. Robert Austin,
P.O. Box 4536, Des Moines, IA 50336.